# THE Desert Encampments

MOSAICA PRESS

# THE Desert

FROM SINAI
TO THE
HOLY LAND

# Encampments

## ALEXANDER HOOL

Published by Mosaica Press, Inc.
www.mosaicapress.com
info@mosaicapress.com

RABBI AHARON FELDMAN
421 YESHIVA LANE, Apt 3A, BALTIMORE, MD 21208
Tel.: 410-6539433  Fax: 410-6534694
Study: 410-4847200 Ext. 6050
E-MAIL: RAF@NIRC.EDU

Rosh Hayeshiva
Ner Israel Rabbinical College

ראש הישיבה
ישיבת נר ישראל

בס"ד

TO WHOM IT MAY CONCERN:

I have seen the book by Rabbi Alex Hool, *The Desert Encampments: From Sinai to the Holy Land,* which traces the encampments (*masa'os*) of the Jewish people in their wanderings from Har Sinai until their entry into Eretz Yisroel. The book seeks to identify the location of these encampments based on the words of Chazal and Rishonim, and supported by satellite photography, authoritative maps and the current Arab names of these locations, often remarkably similar to their names in the Torah. All of this is accompanied by lucidly anno-tated and detailed maps.

The book brings to life the travels of our ancestors in the Desert and explains many obscure *pesukim* in the Torah. Everyone who reads it will find it enlightening, enjoyable and intriguing. By its very nature, the book has many conjectures, all of them reasonable and all of which fall within the purview of what Chazal say about these encampments.

I wish the author much success in disseminating his work.

With respect,
Aharon Feldman

אשר זעליג וייס

כגן 8
פעיה"ק ירושלם ת"ו

בה

ראה ראיתי את ספרו הנפלא של הרה"ג המצוייין ר' אליעזר הול שליט"א על
מ"ב המסעות של בני ישראל במדבר. סוגיא זו עמומה, וכדומני שמקום הניחו
מן השמים למחבר ספר דידן להתגדר בו.
הספר בנוי ומושתת על מקורות מכתבי הקודש בתורה ונביאים וכתובים ועל דברי
חז"ל, והמחבר מראה בקיאות עצומה במקורות אלה.
ספר זה נכתב בשפה האנגלית לתועלת אחינו בני מדינות הים.
ברכתי להרה"ג שליט"א שהוא ת"ח עצום ומרביץ תורה שיזכה עוד רבות להגדיל
תורה ולהאדירה בשמחה שלוה ונחת.

# Table of Contents

# Preface

In the book *Searching for Sinai*, we endeavored to trace the footsteps of the Israelites from their monumental and spectacular exit from Egypt, through to their miraculous entry into the Red Sea, and their onward journey until their eventual encampment at Mount Sinai in Horeb, the site of the receiving of the Torah and the greatest revelation in the history of man. In the course of our study, we were aided by cryptic Scripture, ancient Rabbinic Tradition, simulated satellite imagery, and a detailed topographical study of the area.

Following the precise path taken by the Israelites, comprising **eleven encampments**, we were led to a site for the Biblical Horeb deep into Saudia Arabia, off the coast of the Red Sea. We discovered that incredibly, the name has been maintained for thousands of years and is still called today Horeba. Furthermore, we discovered that the name of the adjacent mountain, Jebel Harb, matches with Mount Horeb, the original name of Mount Sinai, and its characteristics and dimensions fit perfectly with the information derived from the Biblical narrative as well as Rabbinic Tradition.

In the present study, we will continue where we left off and attempt to follow the footsteps of the Israelites from Mount Sinai/Jebel Harb through a further **thirty-one** encampments until their eventual arrival at the border of the Holy Land. We will attempt to trace their initial journey toward the Land of Canaan, and then try to follow the precise path taken by the Israelites after the Sin of the Spies, throughout their forty-year wandering in the wilderness and until their eventual arrival at the straits of Moab by the Jordan River, the final encampment before their entry into the Holy Land.

The Torah goes into very great detail about the travels and events that took place in this period, but the time, place, and details of many of the events are hidden between the profound words of the verses. The identity of the various locations has also remained concealed in cryptic Scripture for thousands of years, and all together leaves us with a blurred picture and understanding of this crucial period in Biblical and Jewish history.

In our day and age, however, access to detailed and accurate mapping of the area as well as penetrating satellite imagery, combined with a meticulous study of the text and fortified with added details from Rabbinic Tradition, allows for the opportunity to unlock the subtle and intriguing Scripture, and fathom the events, the journeys, and the significance of the Desert Encampments.

A central foundation block to understanding what, when, and why things happened is first to ascertain where things happened, and for that we need to identify the location of each and every one of the encampments.

Indeed, we will discover that despite the fact that more than three thousand years that have passed since the trek through the wilderness, the Torah still affords us with crucial information throughout the description of the Israelite sojourns, enabling us to pinpoint today the precise location of the encampments.

This leads to the fascinating revelation that the exile in the wilderness was evidently split up into four separate phases, and we will try to fathom the significance and purpose of these phases. We will also discover that, incredibly, the actual time of "wanderings" was in essence no longer than a couple of months!

The identity of the encampments will also shed much light on the time, place, and details of many episodes throughout the forty years, such as the story of Korah, the Well of Miriam, the sin of Zelophehad, the Red Heifer, the burial of the six hundred thousand, and the blessings of Balaam. We will also be inspired to elucidate many seemingly obscure and enigmatic verses and further unveil hidden journeys to a concealed Kadesh.

We will further gain insight into the sin at Mei Merivah, the death of Miriam, the Battle at Hormah, the wonderful festival of the 15th of Av, and the three decrees comprised in the exile. We will also be led to the graves of the worshippers of the Golden Calf and the site of the miracle at Nahal Arnon.

We will also discover that crucial interpretations of several verses, which now come to light, have far-reaching implications with regard to the halachic border of Canaan, and the path and purpose of the Ark of the Covenant.

Finally, we will take note of the remarkable individual and collective pattern formed by the five encampments at each and every one of the four phases of the exile.

# Acknowledgments

I thank my faithful study partner at Kollel Ponevezh, Rabbi Pesach Bodenheimer, for spending many hours discussing with me in detail the many issues of the book and directing me to relevant references in Rabbinic literature, as well as adding further insights you will find integrated into the work.

Ronnie Halibard very graciously took upon his shoulders the yoke of producing the map pictures from a master map created by Darrel Mordechai, and his skill and expertise is readily visible and adorns the publication.

I am grateful to my brother R' Doniel for his help and proficiency in studying the satellite maps to assist in the location of the site of the miracle of Nahal Arnon, and for his Duke of Edinburgh Gold Award map expertise on wild terrain, in tracing the fastest route from one side of the Nahal to the other. I also thank my cousin Jonathan Feldman for taking screenshot photos of the site, and to my niece Hadassah Hool for her technical assistance.

My sincere gratitude to the *roshei yeshivah* HaRav Aharon Feldman and HaRav Asher Weiss for so kindly taking off their precious time to read through the work and for their warm words of approbation. I also thank my teacher HaRav Michoel Bodenheimer for his wise counsel and very gracious assistance, and my nephew Shneiur Volpo for his kind help.

Once again, I thank Rabbi Doron Kornbluth for his penetrating edit and Rav Yaacov Haber and the Mosaica team for their competence and efficiency and yet another exquisite design.

I am ever indebted to my dear father for his continued interest in my work and for very kindly sponsoring the publication.

Finally, my appreciation to my dear wife for her continued support and for making it possible for me to engage in this study.

## CHAPTER ONE

# Journeying toward the Holy Land

After spending almost a year at Mount Sinai in Horeb, the Israelites, led by the Ark of the Covenant and the Clouds of Glory, set off northward heading for the Land of Canaan. According to the conclusions of *Searching for Sinai*, they began their journey deep into Saudi Arabia, from Horeba just off the shores of the Red Sea at the bottom of its eastern arm.

—————————— Encampment 12[1] ——————————
## KIVROTH HATAAVAH (1)[2]

Biblical Reference: Numbers 10:33, 11:4–34, 33:16

Timeline: 2nd year from Exodus, 20th of Iyar, the 2nd month[3]

Journey: The Israelites leave Horeb/Horeba and the wilderness of Sinai, heading toward the Amorite mountain[4] just west of the bottom of the Dead Sea.[5] They travel for three days,[6] and then arrive in Kivroth Hataavah[7] on the 22nd of the 2nd month,[8] and reside there for one month.[9] This was the 12th encampment from Egypt.

## Event

The Mixed Multitudes[10] who joined with the Israelites incite the Israelites to unduly complain to Moses that they want meat. The Almighty then sends a migration of quail

1 The 12th encampment from Egypt.
2 The 1st encampment from Sinai.
3 Numbers 10:11.
4 Deuteronomy 1:19.
5 Numbers 13:21 and 34:3, and Deuteronomy 1:24.
6 Numbers 10:33.
7 They passed by Taveirah before arriving in Kivroth Hataavah but evidently did not stop off there, and that is why it is not listed as one of the encampments in Numbers 33. *Midrash Aggadah* (quoted in *Rashi*, Numbers 11:1) says that they came to Taveirah at the end of the three days, so evidently, it was just outside Kivroth Hataavah.
8 *Taanis* 29a.
9 Numbers 11:20.
10 *Sifrei*, Numbers 11:4.

11   Quoted in *Rashi*, Numbers 10:33.

12   *Pesachim* 94a.

13   One Hebraic mile is 2,000 cubits. 1 cubit = 6 *tefachim* = 24 finger-breadths = the length of an average arm (from the elbow until the tip of the middle finger) = approximately the length of 48 barley grains = 47.5 cm. See *Rambam, Hilchos Sefer Torah* 9:9. A similar figure can be attained from *Rambam, Hilchos Eruvin* 1:12, based on the average weight of barley grains. This figure is also in line with the implication from *Chullin* 50b and *Bechoros* 38a, which infer that the circumference of the silver Neron Caesar coin, Italian Pundian coin, and Talmudic Sela, is 1 *tefach*. There are many such coins extant today with a diameter of approximately 2.5 cm. (See *Sefer Middos U'Mishkelos shel Torah*, pp. 17, 161, and 166.) See also our *Kuntress Siur Hashiurim* for a detailed discussion and further qualifica- tion of precisely 1.98 cm for 1 fingerbreadth based on the correlation of traditional Rabbinic measurements with modern-day calculations, for the circumference of the earth and the distance from the sun.

14   *Berachos* 54b. See further qualification in chapter 20.

that descends on the camp, but after eating from them for thirty days, many die. At the same time, seventy elders are chosen, and Divine inspiration is bestowed upon them.

## Location

On this particular journey, the Israelites did not travel at a regular speed. *Midrash Aggadah*[11] states that they went three times the normal speed.

- The average pace of walking is 40 Hebraic miles in one day[12] and 3 times that is 120 Hebraic miles (40 × 3 = 120).
- If the Israelites traveled like that for 3 days, they would have covered 360 Hebraic miles (120 × 3 = 360) which is 342 km.[13]

They were not hampered by the ups and downs of the mountainous region in the wilderness because the hills and mountains were flattened as the Ark of the Covenant passed before them,[14] and therefore Kivroth Hataavah must be lo-

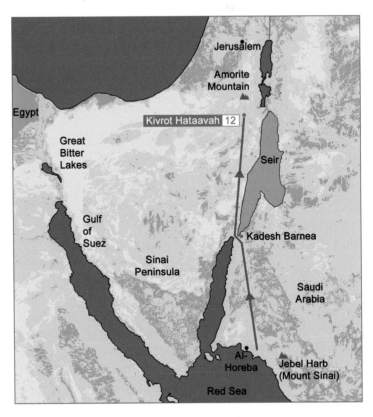

cated at a straight distance from Horeb of 342 km,[15] in a direction toward the southwest corner of the Dead Sea. This takes us right up to the pools of the Dead Sea on its southern tip.

─────────── Encampment 13 ───────────
# HATZEIROTH (2)

Biblical Reference: Numbers 33:17

Timeline: 2nd year from Exodus, 22nd of Sivan, the 3rd month[16]

Journey: The Israelites leave Kivroth Hataavah and arrive at Hatzeiroth on the selfsame day.[17]

## Event

Miriam contracts leprosy after speaking against Moses and is placed in solitary confinement outside the camp. Out

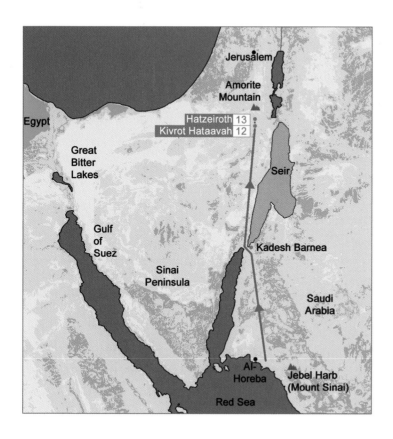

15    See chapter 15 for further qualification.

16    *Taanis* 29a. Indeed, this can be seen on our map as we can see that Kivroth Hataavah is very close to the south-western corner of the Dead Sea, which was the place where they sent out the spies (Numbers 13:16, 21, and 34:3), and the encampment after Hatzeiroth, so the encampment of Hatzeiroth must have been in-between the two, and definitely within one day's journey from Kivroth Hataavah.

17    Ibid.

of respect, the Israelites stay in Hatzeiroth for seven days, awaiting her return before moving on.[18]

## Location

Since the Israelites reach Hatzeiroth within one day, Hatzeiroth must be right next to Kivroth Hataavah, and indeed when we consult a detailed map of the area, we find a mountain there called Mount Hatzeirah, and nearby the River Hatzeirah.[19]

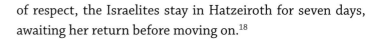

## Encampment 14
# RITHMAH (3)

**Biblical Reference:** Numbers 12:16, 13:26, 33:18

**Timeline:** 2nd year from Exodus, 29th of Sivan, the 3rd month

**Journey:** The Israelites leave Hatzeiroth and arrive at Rithmah, also called Kadesh[20] (and later called Kadesh Barnea in Numbers 32:80).

## Event

On the same day they arrive,[21] spies are sent out to explore the Land of Canaan.[22] The spies return 40 days later[23] on the 8th of Av[24] and try to dissuade the people from entering Canaan. That night, the people weep and seek to return to Egypt. This results in the prohibition of entering the Land, the decree of wandering in the wilderness for 40 years, and the death in these ensuing years of the males of that generation above 20 years old and under 60.[25] The 9th of Av becomes a day of tribulations for the Jewish people. On this day, both the first and second Temples are destroyed[26] and many other troubles and grievances befall the Jewish people on this day, throughout history.[27]

## Location

We know from Numbers 13:21, 33:36, and 34:3, and Deuteronomy 1:24, that Kadesh/Rithmah is next to the southwestern corner of the Dead Sea. Indeed, when we turn

18  Numbers 12:15.
19  The name Hatzeiroth, which is actually the plural form of Hatzeirah, may have been called so because the place is next to the river and the mountain.
20  Numbers 13:26.
21  *Taanis* 29a.
22  Numbers 13.
23  Ibid., 13:25.
24  *Taanis* 29a.
25  *Bava Basra* 121b.
26  *Seder Olam*, chap. 30.
27  For example: the crushing of the Bar Kochba revolt and the destruction of the city of Beitar in 132 CE; the beginning of the first Crusade that killed 10,000 people in the first month, in 1035 CE; the expulsion from England in 1290 CE; the expulsion from Spain in 1492 CE; the beginning of the First World War in 1914 CE; and the deportation of the Warsaw ghetto to the Treblinka concentration camp in 1942 CE.

to the map of the area we find a place called Rothem just off the southwest corner of the Dead Sea and just north of Hatzeiroth.

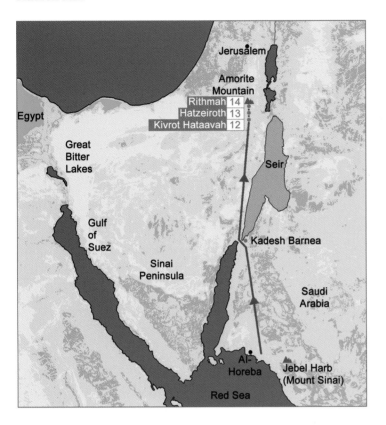

## CHAPTER TWO

# The Hidden Journey to Kadesh

Following the Sin of the Spies, we are told in Deuteronomy[1] that the Israelites resided in Kadesh for many days. The simple understanding is that they stayed where they were at Rithmah/Kadesh, but as we will see, that was not the case.

————————— Encampment 15 —————————
## KADESH (4)

Biblical Reference: **Numbers 33:18**

Timeline: **2nd year from Exodus, 10th of Av, the 5th month**[2]

Journey: **The Israelites leave Rithmah at the start of the period of wandering and arrive in Rimon Paretz.**[3]

## Problem

- Following the Sin of the Spies, the Israelites are instructed to leave Kadesh/Rithmah the very next day in Numbers 14:25.
- This is problematic, as in Deuteronomy 1:46 the verse says that following the Sin of the Spies, the Israelites resided in Kadesh for *"many days."*
- The problem is further aggravated by the qualification of *Seder Olam*, which deduces from the continuation of the verse that they stayed in Kadesh for *19 years*,[4] whereas the verse in Deuteronomy 2:14 says

1   1:46.
2   Numbers 14:25.
3   This pronunciation, used here and hereafter, is the way it is pronounced in the Torah. However, as pointed out by Rabbi Binyomin Prenzlau, it might be pronounced that way because the note under the word *"Paretz"* is an *esnachta*, in which case the natural pronunciation would be *"Rimon Peretz."*
4   *Seder Olam*, chap. 8.

that *38 years elapsed* from the time they left Kadesh Barnea until they passed Nahal Zared.

- This would indicate that the Israelites wandered in the wilderness for *57 years*, but the verse in Numbers 32:13 clearly states that they were in the wilderness for just 40 years.

## Solution

The answer to this vexing problem is actually hidden in the words of Rabbinic Tradition.

- *Seder Olam* in the same place states that the number of encampments in the wilderness totaled 42.[5]
- However, when we look at the list in Numbers 33, we find only 41 encampments.
- *Rashi* helps us out a little bit by stating that there were 20 encampments between Rithmah until the death of Aaron at Hor Hahar, although the verse lists just 19, so evidently the missing encampment lay between Rithmah and Hor Hahar.

The hidden encampment is actually hinted to in the cryptic words of *Seder Olam*. After stating the time spent in Kadesh, *Seder Olam* concludes that from here we see that the number of encampments totaled 42. Evidently, what *Seder Olam* is trying to tell us is that the Kadesh that the Israelites resided in for "many days" was not the same Kadesh/Kadesh Barnea where they sent out the spies.[6]

There were in fact two places called Kadesh.

- Edom was situated on Mount Se'ir,[7] and is the stretch of mountain that extends from the corner of the Dead Sea down to Eilath and Etzion Gaver by the Gulf of Aqaba on the tip of the eastern arm of the Red Sea, as indicated in Deuteronomy 2:8 and Kings I 9:26.
- One Kadesh was situated by the southwestern corner of the Dead Sea, as we saw in the previous chapter, but there was another Kadesh situated on the southern corner of Edom.

5   This is actually hinted to in the words of Joshua in Numbers 11:27, when he tells Moses that Eldad and Meidad prophesied of Moses's death. The words he used were "מתנבאים במחנה," which is an anagram of the words "נביא מת מחנה מב," which means "[the] prophet dies at the 42nd encampment."

6   Numbers 13:26, 32:8.

7   Genesis 36:9, 16.

- In Numbers 20:14, Moses sends messengers to the king of Edom from Kadesh on the corner of Edom,[8] requesting permission to pass through his land in order to enter the Land of Canaan.
- Obviously then, this Kadesh was on the southern corner of Edom.
- After being refused passageway at Kadesh, the Israelites had to circle the border of Edom (Judges 11:18) indicating that Kadesh lay on the southwestern corner of Edom, which lies next to the Red Sea, and indeed this is also indicated in Judges 11:16.
- The *Rambam* writes that this Kadesh was also called Kadesh Barnea,[9] like the northern Kadesh, and it is this Kadesh Barnea that Moses refers to in Deuteronomy 1:2.
- In *Searching for Sinai*,[10] based on this verse and the verse in Numbers 10:33, we found remarkable geographical and mathematical synchronization for the

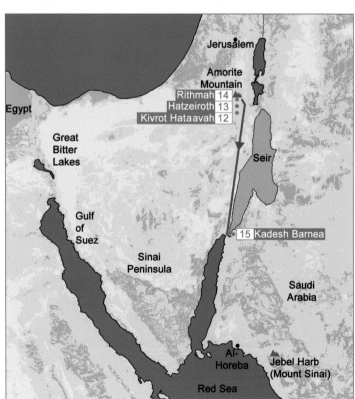

8   Literally, "at the end of the border of Edom."
9   *Moreh Nevuchim* 3:50.
10  Chapters 20 and 21.

distance between Mount Horeb/Jebel Harb and this Kadesh Barnea.

Indeed, the Israelites left the northern Kadesh Barnea, situated on the southwestern corner of the Dead Sea, the very next day, on the 10th of Av, as instructed, but they then traveled to the southern Kadesh Barnea, next to the Red Sea at the tip of the Gulf of Aqaba, and here they resided for 19 years.

*Seder Olam* then tells us that when we add this second Kadesh Barnea to the list of encampments mentioned in Numbers 33, we then get a total of 42 encampments.

Why this encampment is not mentioned explicitly in Numbers 33 like all the others can be explained simply: all the other encampments referred to are described as being "in the list of journeys," since the encampments were of a temporary nature, whereas this encampment, which was of a fixed nature lasting for 19 years,[11] does not belong in that category.[12]

11 *Malbim*, based on *Midrash Rabbah Vayikra* 10:5 explains that through the merit of prayer and repentance, the 38 years of wandering were halved to only 19 years. Although we will see later that they also stayed in Yotvathah for 19 years, that was in the period of wandering and was considered of a temporary nature since throughout their stay there, they did not know if the next day they would be on the move again.

12 In chapter 22, we will discover further that this Kadesh Barnea appears in several other places in the Bible, but each time the Torah mysteriously seems to make efforts to hide it from the naked eye. We will try to understand why.

CHAPTER THREE

# The First Stage of the Exile

After staying 19 years at Kadesh, the Israelites traveled to four different locations in a very short space of time. We will see that the fifth location was none other than Mount Sinai itself, which evidently culminated the first stage of the exile.

Encampment 16

## RIMON PARETZ (5)

Biblical Reference: Numbers 33:19

Timeline: 21st year from Exodus[1]

Journey: The Israelites leave the southern Kadesh Barnea and travel to Rimon Paretz.

## Location

We know from Deuteronomy 2:1–3 that most of the wanderings of the Israelites were around Mount Se'ir, so the first place to look is around that area, and with a casual glance at the map a very likely candidate is already forthcoming.

To the west of Mount Se'ir lies a place called Rimon and next to it lies a gigantic crater, which can be taken as the translation of Pirtzah in Hebrew, and hence the name Rimon Paretz.

---

1    *Seder Olam*, chap. 8.

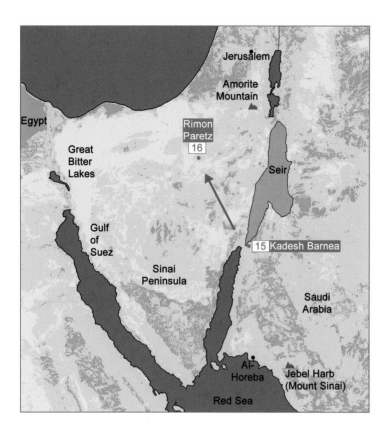

---
— Encampment 17 —
# LIVNAH (6)

Biblical Reference: **Numbers 33:20**

Timeline: **21st year from Exodus[2]**

Journey: **The Israelites leave Rimon Paretz and travel to Livnah.**

## Location

Livnah (לבנה) is also mentioned in Kings II 8:22, and the implication from the verse there is that it lies to the west of Se'ir and south of the Land of Judah.

Indeed, about 90 km northwest of our location of Rimon Paretz, there is a mountain called Jebel Libni (לבני).[3]

2   See chapter 21.

3   It is also interesting to note that the numerical value of the letters הר לבני (Jebel Libni) amounts to the same numerical value of the letters "מקום זה הוא לבנה" which means "this place is Livnah."

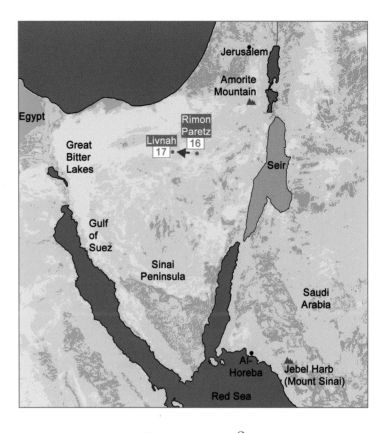

---------- Encampment 18 ----------
# RISAH (7)

Biblical Reference: Numbers 33:21

Timeline: 21st year from Exodus[4]

Journey: The Israelites leave Livnah and travel to Risah.

## Location

In the area surrounding Se'ir, there is just one place with a name synonymous with Risah and that is the River Rasiya in modern-day Jordan.[5] Rasiya is situated to the south-east of Se'ir.

4 This encampment, as well as all the following encampments until Yotvathah, were all in the 21st year, as will be explained later in chapter 11.

5 It is fascinating to note that *Targum Yonasan* (Numbers 33:21) says on this verse that they encamped "בבית ריסה" (literally, "in the house of Risah"), which is an anagram of the words "סביב רתיה," which means "around Rasiya."

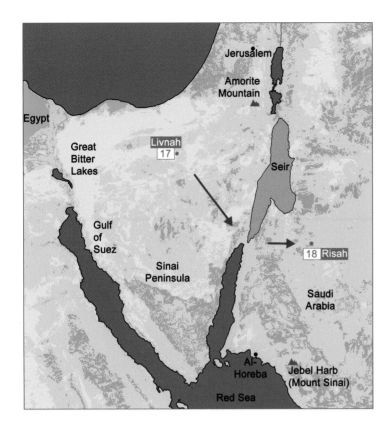

---
### Encampment 19
# KEHEILATHAH (8)

Biblical Reference: Numbers 33:22, 16, 17:1–15.

Timeline: 21st year from Exodus

Journey: The Israelites leave Risah and journey to Keheilathah.

## Event

At this point, the argument of Korah erupts[6] and results in the death of the 250 incense-bringers, and the whole assembly of Korah is swallowed up into the ground. The following day, the people complain to Moses and a plague breaks out. Under Moses's instruction, Aaron runs to the center of the assembly with fire and incense—and the plague abates, leaving fourteen thousand dead.[7]

[6] Indicated by *Targum Yonasan*, who says this was the place where the dispute broke out.

[7] This now alleviates a problem raised by the *Rashbam* in *Bava Basra* 119a. *Seder Olam*, chap. 8, says that the episode of Korah took place after the Sin of the Spies. The straightforward understanding is that *Seder Olam* means that the episode took place as a consequence of the decree following the Sin of the Spies. Accordingly, 38 years later, at the end of the exile, the orphans of the plague must have been at least 38 years old. Yet the Talmud in *Bava Basra* takes the position that they were under twenty! However, in light of *Targum Yonasan* above, this is now answered. Indeed, the episode of Korah took place after the Sin of the Spies, but not straight away—only 20 years later at Keheilathah. Thus, the newly born children of those who died in the plague were under 20 at the time of the entrance into Canaan.

## Location

To the southwest of Risah, about 180 km away, we find a town with a similar-sounding name, **Qalas**, which means "fortress." This identification is further corroborated by *Targum Yonasan*,[8] which we will see later indicates that there was another Keheilathah due south of this one. Indeed, we find another **Qalas** about 60 km to the southeast.[9]

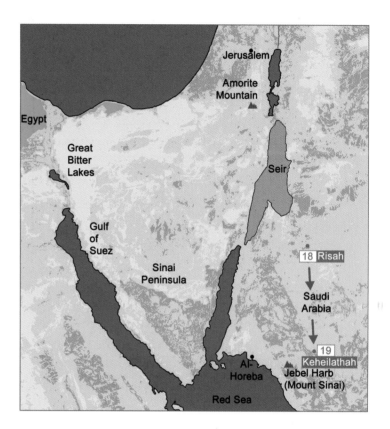

8    Numbers 33:26.

9    The northern one is called Kalas el Achdar and the southern one is called Kalas el Muazam.

## CHAPTER FOUR

# The Korah Conflagration

An intriguing question that now comes to the fore is why, after 20 years, did the argument of Korah suddenly flare up? The verse describes Korah challenging the authority of Moses and Aaron,[1] but why now and not 20 years earlier? The location of Keheilathah, together with a crucial *Midrash Tanchuma*, now allows us to piece things together.

- After the sin of the Golden Calf, the service in the Tabernacle was taken away from the firstborns and given to the Levites.[2]
- *Midrash Tanchuma*[3] tells us that the argument broke out after the Levites were instructed to cut off all their hair and were waved in the air by Aaron in a cleansing and atoning process in preparation for service in the Tabernacle.[4]
- Korah, being the oldest, was first in line and felt very embarrassed after the procedure of having all his hair shaven off and being lifted in the air by Aaron. This sparked off his immediate response of challenging the validity of Moses and Aaron.
- The location of Keheilathah, Qalas, happens to be just east of Jebel Harb—our recently discovered Mount Horeb/Sinai.

We can now surmise that after the 19 years of repentance and the ensuing encampments that constituted the first phase of the exile, the Israelites were now ready to begin the Temple service with their Levite substitutes in the very place

1    Numbers 16:3.
2    Ibid. 3:41, and Deuteronomy 10:8.
3    *Parashas Korach* 3.
4    This might be hinted to in the name Keheilathah which in Hebrew is קהלתה. This has the same letters as הקהלת, which means "you have assembled," and is used in the instruction to cleanse and atone the Levites in front of the Israelites in Numbers 8:9.

where it should have begun—at Mount Sinai. Thus, just next to Mount Sinai, they encamped and were instructed to cleanse the Levites and atone for them in preparation for this.

The embarrassment felt by Korah in the cleansing process caused him to suspect whether it was indeed ordered by Divine instruction. This then led to him challenging the appointment of Aaron as High Priest, and the authority of Moses as a whole.

## CHAPTER FIVE

# The Red Heifer

In Numbers 19, Moses is instructed to take a Red Heifer and give it to Elazar the deputy High Priest to slaughter outside the camp, and then to burn the carcass. The ashes were to be used in a cleansing process for those who had become unclean by contact with a dead person.

When did this take place?

According to *Sifri*,[1] this took place at the time of the consecration of the Tabernacle on the 2nd of Nissan in the 2nd year following the Exodus.

However, there appears to be another opinion among the Sages.

- In Numbers 9:7 in Nissan of the 2nd year, a number of people came to Moses asking how they could offer the Paschal lamb, since they were unclean from having come into contact with a dead person.
- Rabbi Jose from Gallil says that these were the men who carried the coffin of Joseph. Rabbi Akiva says that they were Mishael and Eltzaphan, who took out Nadav and Avihu after they died in the Tabernacle on the day it was consecrated.[2]
- Rabbi Isaac rejects both these views as they would have had time to engage in the seven-day cleansing process before the time due for the Paschal offering, and therefore he says that they must have been those who were involved in a burial within seven days before.

1    Numbers 7:1.
2    Leviticus 10:4.

We can now elucidate the view of Rabbi Jose and Rabbi Akiva.

Part of the cleansing process of the Levites was to be sprinkled with the ashes of the Red Heifer.[3]

Evidently, the view of Rabbi Jose and Rabbi Akiva is that the Red Heifer was not burned in the 2nd year, but at the time when the ashes were needed to cleanse the Levites in preparation for service in the Tabernacle, which took place 20 years later at Keheilathah, in accordance with *Midrash Tanchuma* and *Targum Yonasan*. Since there were no ashes in the 2nd year, the carriers of Joseph's coffin and Mishael and Eltzaphan would have not been able to cleanse themselves.

This would now explain why Mishael and Eltzaphan, who were Levites,[4] were instructed to take out the corpses of Nadav and Avihu and not their brothers Elazar and Ithamar. Elazar and Ithamar were Kohanim (priests), and they were needed in the Tabernacle service. Had they become unclean they would have been prohibited from entering the Tabernacle for the duration of the next 20 years until they would be sprinkled with the ashes of the Red Heifer.[5]

We can now understand why the portion of the Red Heifer is placed next to the portion of Korah as they both took place at the same time.

This might also explain why the portion of Pesach Sheini (the second opportunity to bring the Paschal Lamb) is put next to the portion of the cleansing of the Levites in preparation for the Tabernacle service.[6] The portion of Pesach Sheini was introduced after the unclean men expressed their despondency to Moses about not being able to offer the Paschal lamb. The juxtaposition of the two portions might be to hint that the reason why they remained unclean was because the unusual birth of a Red Heifer was only instigated by Divine Providence when it was crucial, i.e., at the time when it was needed to facilitate the cleansing process of the Levites in order to inaugurate them for the Tabernacle service.[7]

3    Numbers 8:7.
4    Exodus 6:22.
5    Pointed out by Rabbi Pesach Bodenheimer.
6    Numbers 8 and 9.
7    Although these men were still unclean at the time of Pesach Sheini, they were still allowed to offer their sacrifice then, in accordance with the view of Rabbi Judah in *Pesachim* 95b that the Pesach Sheini can be offered whilst being unclean.

## CHAPTER SIX

# Har Shafer

---

Encampment 20

## HAR SHAFER (9)

Biblical Reference: **Numbers 33:23, 17:16–25**

Timeline: **21st year from Exodus**

Journey: The Israelites leave Keheilathah and travel to Har Shafer.

## Event

Just after the plague abides, Moses is instructed to place the staffs of all the princes of the twelve tribes in the Tabernacle to reveal who is the chosen one. The next morning, the staff of Levi with the name of Aaron engraved upon it blossoms and brings forth almonds. *Targum Yonasan*[1] says that the name Shafer, which means "beautiful," alludes to the fruits that grew there. In the light of the above, it would seem that the miracle of Aaron's staff took place here at Mount Shafer, and this is what *Targum Yonasan* is hinting to.

## Location

*Midrash Tanchuma*[2] states that all the mountains of the wilderness in front of the Israelites were flattened except for just three: Mount Sinai, Mount Nebo, and Hor Hahar, as indicated by the verses[3] that describe them as "mountains" at the time they encamped there. This raises a question, as

---

1   Numbers 33:23.
2   Numbers, *Parashas Chukas* 14.
3   Exodus 19:2, Numbers 33:37, Deuteronomy 34:1.

there is seemingly one other encampment by a mountain[4]—Mount Shafer mentioned above. So why is this not also listed by the midrash?

The answer now becomes apparent, as we have seen that Keheilathah is right next to Mount Sinai/Jebel Harb. All the "non-flat" mountains *were* mentioned. The midrash does not include Mount Shafer as a fourth mountain that was not flattened because it takes the position that Mount Shafer is actually referring to Mount Sinai, which is evidently called Mount Shafer after the "*imrei shefer*—words of beauty" that were given on it.

We can also now infer a straightforward meaning to the words "Mount Shafer." Jebel Harb is also just next to a mountain range called Jebel **Shifa**. Evidently, they camped there, by the flattened Jebel "Shifa," but the Torah refers to the encampment as "Mount Shafer" because it was also located next to Mount Sinai/Shafer.

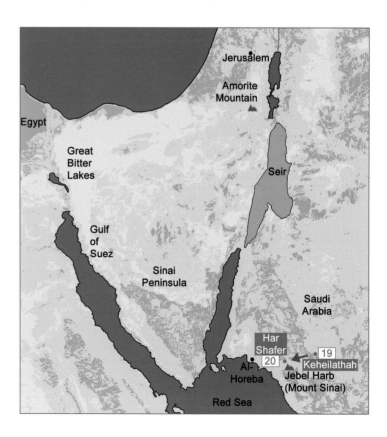

4    We will see later that Harei Ha'avarim is actually referring to Mount Nebo.

## CHAPTER SEVEN

# Haradah

Biblical Reference: Numbers 33:24, 17:27–28, 18:1–7

Timeline: 21st year from Exodus[1]

Journey: The Israelites leave Mount Shafer and journey to Haradah.

## Location

Just northeast of our location of Mount Shafer lies the River Ahadar, which seems to be synonymous with Haradah. The word *haradah*, which means "fear," is perhaps a play on the name Ahadar and is adapted to refer to the fear that took place there. *Targum Yonasan*[2] says that the name Haradah is alluding to the fear of death expressed by the Israelites at this encampment.

## Event

In Numbers 17:27, the Israelites inform Moses that they are scared of dying by overstepping their mark of restriction and entering the Tabernacle itself, a prohibition that carried with it the death penalty. In response, the Almighty tells Aaron that the responsibility of making sure no unauthorized person draws near the Tabernacle and the holy vessels is given over to the Kohanim and Levites.[3]

1   See chapter 21.
2   Numbers 33:24.
3   Ibid., 18:1–7.

This portion is written just after the Torah describes the episode of the staff of Aaron bringing forth almonds, which we have learned took place at Mount Shafer.

Evidently, this took place at the next encampment, Haradah. Why were the fears of the Israelites expressed only now?

This can now be understood as only shortly before, in Keheilathah, the Israelites were given the order to cleanse and atone the Levites in preparation for their service in the Tabernacle and were informed of the death penalty for anyone (other than Kohanim) entering the Tabernacle.[4]

Furthermore, at the previous encampment, the staff of Aaron with the blossom and almonds was left in the Tabernacle as testimony to his Divine appointment,[5] and they may have now had the added concern that out of curiosity to catch a glimpse of the miraculous staff, they might overstep their mark.

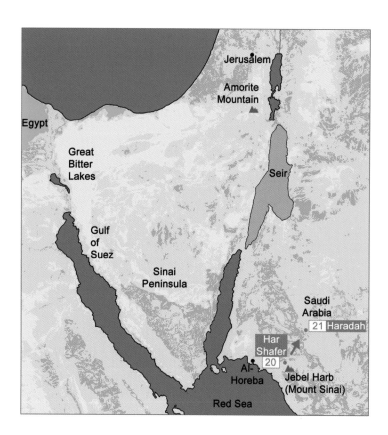

---

4    Ibid., 8:19.
5    Ibid., 17:25.

## CHAPTER EIGHT

# Makheiloth

---

Encampment 22

## MAKHEILOTH (II)

Biblical Reference: Numbers 33:25, 18:8–24

Timeline: 21st year from Exodus

Journey: The Israelites leave Haradah and journey
to Makheiloth.

## Location

The *Baal Haturim* says that Makheiloth is one and the same as Keheilathah, which we have identified as Qalas. Keheilathah means "assembly," and Makheiloth can infer "one who gathers assemblies." This can now be understood because they originally went there for the assembly to cleanse and atone for the Levites, hence the name Keheilathah; but following that assembly, Korah gathered together two other assemblies against Moses and Aaron,[1] hence the name Makheiloth in the plural form—with the emphasis on the gatherer (Korah).

## Event

Just after the verse relates the transmission to Aaron of the responsibility given over to the Kohanim and Levites to prevent unauthorized persons from drawing near to the Tabernacle (which we have identified in the last chapter as having taken place in the previous encampment, Haradah),

1    Numbers 15:3
     and 16:19.

the verse then refers to another audience of Aaron with the Almighty, where he is told of the various contributions stipulated for the Kohanim.[2] This evidently took place at this encampment of Makheiloth, and perhaps was given over here specifically, as an affirmation of the Divine appointment of Aaron in the very place where this appointment was questioned.[3]

Aaron was also told at this point of the tithes given to the Levites as payment for their service in the Tabernacle.[4] This evidently was given here as a continuation of the original plan after atoning for the Levites in their preparation for the service in the Tabernacle.

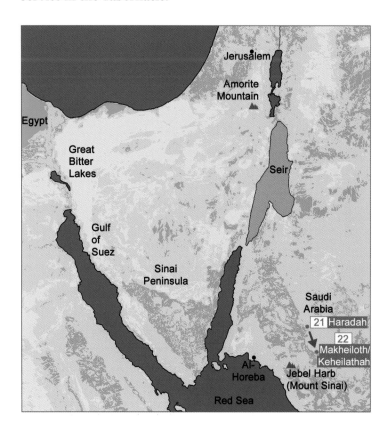

2    Ibid., 18:8–20.
3    See location below.
4    Numbers 18:21–24.

## CHAPTER NINE

# The Second Stage of the Exile

W e will discover that the following five encampments were all places in which the Israelites had previously encamped, but sinned there. Evidently the purpose of these encampments was to return to the place of their sin and atone for it.

## Encampment 23
## THACHATH (12)

Biblical Reference: Numbers 33:26

Timeline: 21st year from Exodus

Journey: The Israelites leave Makheiloth and journey to Thachath.

### Event

Following the laws of the contributions to the Kohanim, given over to Aaron in Numbers 18:8–24, which we have identified as having taken place in Makheiloth, the Almighty speaks to Moses and tells him of the laws of the Levites giving contribution from their tithes to the Kohanim.[1] This evidently took place at a different time and most probably at the next encampment, Thachath.

### Location

*Targum Yonasan*[2] translates Thachath, which means "bottom," to be referring to the lower Makheiloth. We have identified Makheiloth as Qalas el Achdar—and indeed, we

---

1    Numbers 18:25–32.
2    Ibid., 33:26.

find another **Qalas**, Qalas el Muazam, about 60 km to the southeast. Evidently, this is the Biblical Thachath.

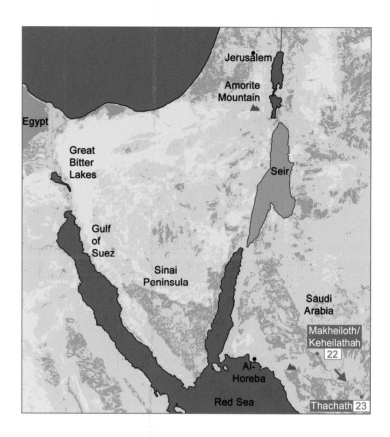

---
Encampment 24
---

# THARACH (13)

Biblical Reference: Numbers 33:27

Timeline: 21st year from Exodus

Journey: The Israelites leave Thachath and journey to Tharach.

## Event

We will discover that the identity of the following three encampments reveal that they were places that the Israelites had encamped in before, but had sinned there, so evidently their return to these places was in order to atone for the sin that took place in the respective locations. At the encampment of Tharach, based on its location below, the Israelites evidently atoned for the sin of complaining they had no water on their way to Sinai.

## Location

The locations of the later encampments include all the places where the Israelites sinned apart for one—Refidim—where the Israelites complained they had no water, so evidently, Tharach must be referring to Refidim. The word Tharach (תרח) has a similar phonetic sound to *sarach* (סרח), which means "sinned" and is also an anagram of *rose'ach* (רתח) meaning "boiling." This possibly alludes to the attack of the Amalekites at Refidim. The *Tanchuma*,[3] based on the verse in Deuteronomy 25:18, compares the Israelites at that time to a boiling bath that no one can enter, but after one evil person jumps in, although he is scalded, the bath is cooled down for others to follow.

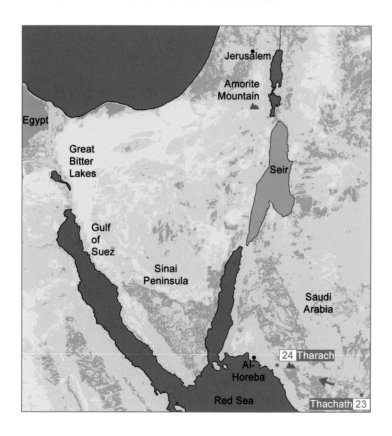

3    *Parashas Ki Seitzei* 9.

We know that Refidim was located just outside Horeb[4] and situated by an expanse of dirty water.[5] In *Searching for Sinai*, we identified it as being by the muddy lake just next to Horeba in Saudi Arabia.

—————————— Encampment 25 ——————————

# MITHKAH (14)

**Biblical Reference:** Numbers 33:28

**Timeline:** 21st year from Exodus

**Journey:** The Israelites leave Tharach and journey to Mithkah.

## Location

Mithkah means "sweet," and *Targum Yonasan*[6] says this is referring to the water there. We find just one place mentioned in the Torah where the water was sweet. This was at

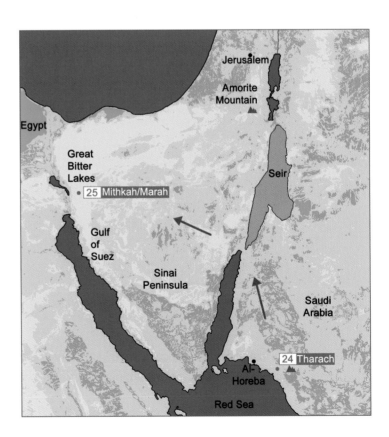

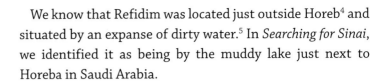

---

4   Exodus 17:6.

5   Ibid., v. 1.

6   Numbers 33:28.

Marah, after Moses threw the wood into the bitter waters referred to in Exodus 15:25. It is thus evidently Marah that the Torah is hinting to by the name Mithkah. It also seems to be a play on the word Mislah, which is the name of the place just next to the Bitter Lakes, north of Suez, which we have already identified in *Searching for Sinai* as Marah, which means "bitter." The verse now calls it Mithkah, meaning "sweet," hinting to the miracle that took place there.

## Event

The Israelites atone for the sin of complaining about the lack of water at Marah.

---

### Encampment 26
# HASHMONAH (15)

Biblical Reference: Numbers 33:29

Timeline: 21st year from Exodus

Journey: The Israelites leave Mithkah and journey to Hashmonah.

## Location

The name Hashmonah has the same numerical value as the name Kadesh,[7] the place of the Sin of the Spies. We will discover later that this is also the place where Miriam died. Indeed, the name Hashmon is given as a title of respect to a person of greatness, as we find in Psalms 68:32,[8] and with Mattathius and his sons—the "Hasmoneans" at the time of the Chanukah story in the mid-Second Temple era. Thus, the name Hashmonah—indicating the feminine form—would be referring to Miriam. Furthermore, the word Hashmonah also has the same numerical value as the words טמון בו מרים, which means "Miriam is buried there."

## Event

The Israelites atone for the sin committed at Kadesh after the spies returned from the Land of Canaan and turned the hearts of the Israelites against entering the Land .

7   The numerical value of Kadesh is 504, whereas the numerical value of Hashmonah is actually 503, but together with the *kollel* (the overall form of the numerical components, often included in numerical equations), it is 504. Furthermore, a variation of Hashmonah is Hashmonaah, which indeed has a numerical value of 504.

8   See *Radak*.

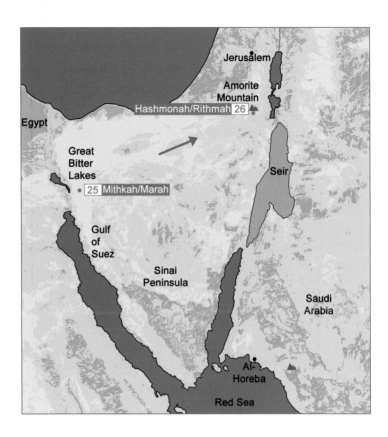

—— Encampment 27 ——
## MOSEIROTH (16)

Biblical Reference: Numbers 33:30

Timeline: 21st year from Exodus

Journey: The Israelites leave Hashmonah and journey to Moseiroth.

### Location

The root of the word Moseiroth is *mussar*, which means "rebuke." *Targum Yonasan*[9] says that at this place, admonition and chastisement were meted out. This is evidently referring to Hatzeiroth,[10] where Miriam was chastised for speaking out against Moses and contracted leprosy. This may also be hinted in the cryptic verse in Deuteronomy 10:6:

• The verse intriguingly says that the Israelites traveled to Moseiroth, and there Aaron died. However, we

9   Numbers 33:30.

10  We have also discovered earlier that Hatzeirah is the location by Mount Hatzeirah and the River Hatzeirah. Indeed, the numerical value of the word Moseiroth (מוסרות) is equal to the numerical value of the words ב' חצרות, which means "two Hatzeiroth."

know from Numbers 20 and 33:38 that Aaron died much later at Hor Hahar.

- This can now be understood as hinting to "the death" of Aaron at Hatzeiroth. In Numbers 12:12, when his sister Miriam contracted leprosy, Aaron implored to Moses on her behalf, claiming that a leper is like a dead person and since Miriam was his relative, he himself was considered partly dead.[11]

## Event

The Israelites atone for the sin of Miriam and for not taking heed of what happened to Miriam. Indeed, their failure to do so resulted in their succumbing to the slander of the spies.

This brings us to the end of the second phase of wanderings of the Israelites during their 40-year exile. There was one other place where the Israelites sinned, Taveirah/Kivroth Hataavah, but the Israelites did not return there, possibly because they were not ready to atone for these sins at the

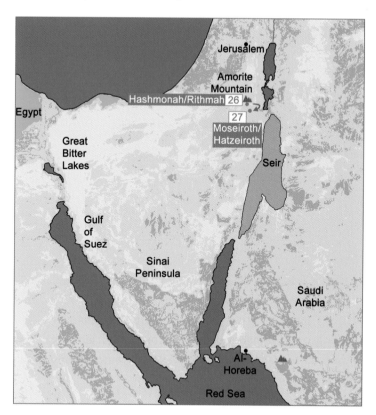

11     Indeed, as pointed out by Rabbi Pesach Bodenheimer, according to the view of Rabbi Akiva in *Shabbos* 97a, Aaron himself contracted leprosy at the time.

time. This would now explain the verse in Deuteronomy 9:22, where Moses, in admonishing the Israelites before he dies, singles out the sins at Taveirah and Kivroth Hataavah.[12]

12  Massah is also mentioned after Taveirah. Refidim was actually called Massah U'Merivah (Exodus 17:7). This can now be explained because when they returned to Refidim (Tharach), they evidently atoned only for the sin of Merivah, which means "quarrel." It was also called Massah, which means "test" because they also tested the Almighty (Exodus 17:7), but they evidently did not atone for this sin. That is why only Massah is mentioned here. Massah is put next to Taveirah as both involved the tribe of Dan who had among them an idol (see *Targum Yonasan*, Exodus 17:8 and Numbers 11:1).

CHAPTER TEN

# The Journey to Thachath

We have seen that after the first phase of the exile, the Israelites came back to Mount Sinai to inaugurate the Levites to the Tabernacle service in place of the firstborns. In the second phase, we saw that the Israelites returned to the places where they had sinned, evidently to atone for the respective sins at the places where they were committed. However, one place, Thachath, the 23rd encampment, does not seem to fit in with this pattern, as we do not know of any sin that occurred there.

Another problem we have is that one place that surprisingly does not seem to be on the list of places is Mount Sinai—to atone for the sin of the Golden Calf.

After the Ten Commandments were given, Moses ascended Mount Sinai and resided there for 40 days. The people misunderstood the time due for his return, and the apparent delay caused unrest, resulting in the formation and worship of the Golden Calf. When Moses was told what happened, he interceded on behalf of the Israelites and saved the nation from being destroyed. Moses then came down the mountain and, upon seeing the Calf and the dancing, he threw the Tablets of stone from his hand and smashed them at the foot of the mountain. Under the instruction of the Almighty, the tribe of Levites put to death by sword about 3,000 sinners. Others died by plague and others after forcefully drinking from the stream strewn with the ashes of the Golden Calf that Moses burned.[1]

1   Exodus 32. *Avodah Zarah* 44a qualifies that those of whom there was testimony that they had been warned died by the sword, those of whom there was testimony only that they had sinned died by plague, and those without any testimony at all against them died by the drinking.

Surely the Israelites should have come back to atone for the Sin of the Golden Calf as well![2]

What seems reasonable to suggest in answer to both questions together is that the Israelites indeed traveled to Thachath to atone for a sin too—the sin of the Golden Calf, as explained below.

- In chapter 9, we identified Thachath with Qalas el Muazam. This location is about 170 km from Mount Sinai/Jebel Harb.
- In Numbers 10:33, the verse says that the Ark of the Covenant went before the Israelites a distance of three days' journey. No doubt the Ark of the Covenant was designated to stay close to the Israelite camp, so we can see from here that the concept of proximity is a distance of a three-day journey.

It was evidently not fitting that those who sinned with the Golden Calf should remain in proximity of Mount Sinai and the Israelite camp. Those who died were therefore taken a distance of a three-day journey away and buried there. A distance walked at an average pace in one day is 40 Hebraic miles and, in haste, 50 Hebraic miles,[3] and for three and a half days,[4] 175 Hebraic miles, which is 166.25 km,[5] which takes us just up to Thachath.

The purpose of the journey of the whole Israelite camp to Thachath nineteen years later was evidently to encamp at the site of the graves of those who died at the Golden Calf, and to atone for the sin. Perhaps this is hinted to in the name Thachath, which means "underneath," alluding to those buried there under the ground.

2    They did return to Mount Sinai, as we saw in chapter 6. However, this encampment was not consecutive with the other 4 mentioned; evidently, the purpose was not to atone but to initiate the Tabernacle service with the Levite substitutes, as mentioned in chapter 4.

3    *Pesachim* 94a.

4    Anything less than half would also have a status of "being three days away" by rounding off to the nearest day.

5    See chapter 1, note 13.

CHAPTER ELEVEN

# The Third Stage of the Exile

The next five encampments were all close together geographically, yet in time extended from the 21st year until the 40th year.

———— Encampment 28 ————
## B'NEI YAAKAN (17)

Biblical Reference: Numbers 33:31

Timeline: 21st year from Exodus

Journey: The Israelites leave Moseiroth and journey to B'nei Yaakan.

## Location

- In Deuteronomy 10:6–8, Moses relates that that the Israelites journeyed from Be'eroth B'nei Yaakan to Moseiroth and that Aaron died there and was buried there, and from there they traveled to Gudgod and then on to Yotvathah, "a land of streams of water."
- The verse is cryptically worded, allowing for the interpretation of the words "there" (written three times) to be referring to either Moseiroth[1] or B'nei Yaakan. However, the natural indication is that all three are referring to the same place, and since we know from Numbers 33:32–33 that the Israelites traveled from B'nei Yaakan to Gudgod and then on to Yotvathah, the straightforward indication is that the third

[1] Indeed, in chapter 9, with regard to Moseiroth, we saw that the word "there" in reference to the death of Aaron may be hinting to "his death" at Moseiroth.

"there" is referring to B'nei Yaakan, and therefore naturally the other two as well.

- However, we know from Numbers 20:22–29 and 33:38 that Aaron was buried at Hor Hahar.
- The two together imply that Be'eroth B'nei Yaakan must be in the same area as Hor Hahar.

Indeed, the words באורת בני יעקן (Be'eroth B'nei Yaakan) are an anagram of the words קברת נביא עניו, which mean "the grave of a humble prophet," and the numerical value of the words בני יעקן (B'nei Yaakan) is equal to the numerical value of the words נטמן נביא הכהן, which mean "buried [here is] the prophet priest."

We know from Numbers 20:23 that Hor Hahar lay on the border of Edom. Edom was situated on Mount Se'ir[2] and, as we mentioned earlier,[3] is the stretch of mountain that extends from the corner of the Dead Sea down to Eilath and Etzion Gaver by the Gulf of Aqaba on the tip of the eastern

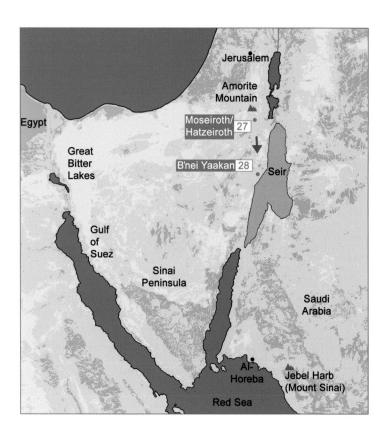

2   Genesis 36:9, 16.

3   Chapter 2.

arm of the Red Sea, as indicated in Deuteronomy 2:8 and Kings I 9:26.

The exact location of Hor Hahar is widely identified as Jebel Harun (Mount Aaron), opposite the ancient city of Petra, which is about 90 km south of our location of Moseiroth. Hor Hahar means the "mountain of the mountain," and *Midrash Tanchuma*[4] explains that it was a mountain on top of a mountain. Indeed, Jebel Harun fits this criterion.

—————— Encampment 29 ——————
## HOR HAGIDGAD (18)

Biblical Reference: **Numbers 33:32, Deuteronomy 10:7**

Timeline: **21st year from Exodus**

Journey: **The Israelites leave B'nei Yaakan and travel to Hor Hagidgad.**

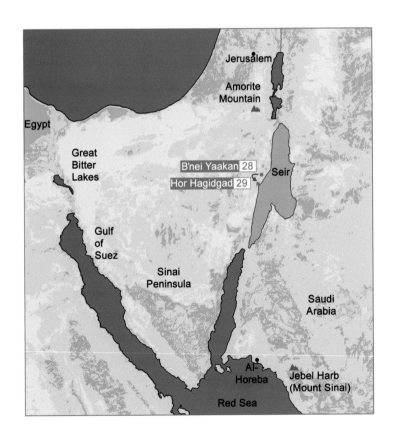

4    Numbers 14.

## Location

In Hebrew the prefix "*ha*" usually denotes the word "the" or "that" and is not usually found at the beginning of a name. Therefore, the word Hagidgad is likely to be a description of the location rather than part of its name. This is also indicated by the omission of the word *hor* in Deuteronomy 10:7 and the slight variation used there: *hagudgodah*.

The word *gud* means "to cut"[5] and, indeed, we find just south of our location of B'nei Yaakan a wadi called Huvar, which cuts across the deep plain between the Dead Sea and the Red Sea. The Hebrew letters for *chor*, חור, can actually be read "*hor*" or "*huvar*," and thus Hor Hagidgad is evidently referring to the Wadi Huvar that cuts across the plain.[6]

───────────── Encampment 30 ─────────────
# YOTVATHAH (19)

Biblical Reference: Numbers 33:33, Deuteronomy 10:7

Timeline: 21st year from Exodus

Journey: The Israelites leave Hor Hagidgad and travel to Yotvathah.

## Location

Just around 15 km south of our location of Hor Hagidgad is a wadi and town still called today Yotvathah.

## Time and Duration of Stay

In Deuteronomy 10:1–11, Moses relates about the rewriting of the Ten Commandments following the sin of the Golden Calf, and in verse 8 says that at that time, the Levites were chosen to carry the Ark, serve in the Tabernacle, and bless the people. However, intriguingly, in verses 6–7, Moses digresses and relates of the death of Aaron at B'nei Yaakan and then about the journey from B'nei Yaakan to Gudgodah and then on to Yotvathah.

In chapter 20, we will learn of the relevance of mentioning the death of Aaron at this point. But this still leaves the enigma of why the journey of B'nei Yaakan to Gudgodah and

5    Gudgod has the same meaning as the word *gud*, just doubled over for emphasis.

6    Indeed, the numerical value of the word חוור (*chuvar*) is equal to the words חר הגד (*chor hagad*), and the numerical value of חר גדגד (*chor gidgad*) is equal to the word בחוור, which means "at Huvar."

on to Yotvathah is mentioned here. Furthermore, why does verse 8, in reverting back to the time of the Sin of the Golden Calf begin with "At that time," which simply implies that it is referring to the time when they arrived at Yotvathah?

We are now in a position to elucidate this cryptic text, and at the same time derive the time and duration of their stay in Yotvathah as well as all the 14 previous encampments.

- We have learned in chapter 5 that the Israelites resided in Kadesh Barnea for 19 years, in repentance, following the Sin of the Spies, and that they then journeyed to Rimon Paretz in the 21st year from the Exodus.
- Three encampments later, at Keheilathah, the Levites were cleansed and atoned in preparation for service in the Tabernacle acting as replacements for the firstborns.
- Accordingly, although the Levites were chosen as replacements immediately after the sin of the Golden Calf, this was only put into practice 19 years later.
- Thus, when verse 8 states that the Levites were "designated at that time," this can carry two meanings: the time of the sin of the Golden Calf when they were chosen, or the time of their appointment 19 years later.

The text is cryptically worded to also imply the second meaning, i.e., the time of their appointment nineteen years later, which was also around the same time that they arrived in Yotvathah.

This means that all the encampments from Keheilathah until Yotvathah took place in the same year, and—following this pattern—evidently, the other three encampments from Rimon Paretz, too, i.e., all in the 21st year from the Exodus. The verse digresses about the journey up until Yotvathah, but no further, in order to point out that all the encampments from Kadesh Barnea until Yotvathah took place around the same time, but the next encampment was not; evidently, they stayed in Yotvathah for a duration of time.

This now explains further why the verse here in Deuteronomy 10:7 specifies that Yotvathah was a land of flowing waters. This is to tell us of the kindness of the Almighty, that the location in which the Israelites were instructed to stay for a long duration was one of very comfortable surroundings.

Since the Torah does not specify exactly how long the Israelites stayed in Yotvathah, the implication is that they stayed there the rest of the 21st year and throughout the next 18 years until the next mentioned date (Numbers 33:38)—the 40th year from the Exodus.[7]

With this, we can now attain insight into the straightforward explanation of the verse in Deuteronomy 2:1, which implies that throughout their stay in the wilderness, the Israelites encircled Mount Se'ir. This can now be understood because throughout almost the entire duration of the Exile, the Israelites resided either in Kadesh Barnea on the south side of Mount Se'ir or in Yotvathah on the west side.

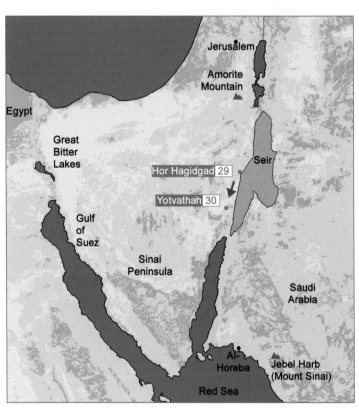

7   It is fascinating to note that the letters of the word יטבתה, with the last three letters expanded (בית, תיו, הא) spell out the words יתבתא הוי יט, which means (in Aramaic) "the stay was 19 (years)."

—————— Encampment 31 ——————
# AVRONAH (20)

Biblical Reference: Numbers 33:34

Timeline: 39th year from Exodus, Nissan, the 1st month[8]

Journey: The Israelites leave Yotvathah and travel
to Avronah.

## Location

About 25 km south of Yotvathah there is a wadi still called
today Avronah.

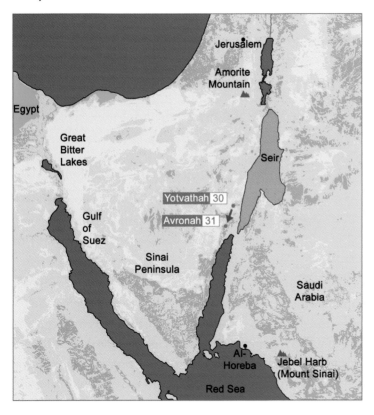

—————— Encampment 32 ——————
# ETZION GAVER (21)

Biblical Reference: Numbers 33:35

Timeline: 39th year from Exodus, Nissan, the 1st month

8    See chapter 21.

Journey: The Israelites leave Avronah and travel to Etzion Gaver.

## Location

We know from Deuteronomy 2:8 that Etzion Gaver is close to Eilath, and from Kings I 9:26 that it lies off the shore of the western arm of the Red Sea. Indeed, the town of Etzion Gaver still exists today next to Eilath at the tip of the Gulf of Aqaba.

## Time and Duration

In Numbers 9:19–20, the verses relate that throughout the sojourn in the wilderness, the duration at each encampment ranged between a few days and many days. Then verses 21–22 specify further that sometimes they stayed just one night, other times a day and a night, two days, a month, or a year.

We have learned earlier in this chapter that the Israelites resided in Kadesh for 19 years, while the ensuing encampments occurred within the space of a few months until they arrived in Yotvathah, where they then stayed up until the 40th year. So where and when did they stay for a duration of one year?

We are left with just two possibilities, and they are the two encampments after Yotvathah: Avronah and Etzion Gaver.

Fascinatingly enough, the names of both encampments seem to hint to the length of time they stayed at them. The letters "בערבנה ויחנו—And they encamped at Avronah" can be rearranged to form the letters ויחנו בעבר נה, which mean "they encamped just over 55," i.e., 56, which is the numerical value of יום, which means "one day."

The letters "ויחנו בעציון גבר—And they encamped at Etzion Gaver" has the numerical value of the words ויחנו ב'ע' שנה, which means "and they camped by the *ayin* (wellspring) for one year."[9]

Since we will see later that the next encampment took place in Nissan of the 40th year, this would mean that sometime in Nissan of the 39th year, they left Yotvathah and

9    In *Searching for Sinai* we discovered that the encampment of Eilim, which had 12 wellsprings (Numbers 33:12) was just by the tip of the Gulf of Aqaba and thus one of the wellsprings could very possibly have been next to Etzion Gaver.

arrived at Avronah, stayed there for a day, and then traveled to Etzion Gaver and stayed there for one year. They then left for the next encampment Kadesh and arrived there in Nissan of the 40th year.[10]

In the next chapter, we will gain insight as to why they stayed at Etzion Gaver for one year.

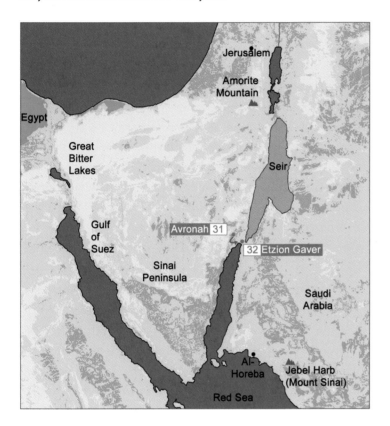

## CHAPTER TWELVE

# The Sin of the Mekoshesh

In the previous chapter, we ascertained that the encampment at Etzion Gaver lasted for one year. This is the only encampment that lasted for a year. Besides for Kadesh and Yotvathah, where they stayed at each for 19 years,[1] all the others were only for a month or less. So, what was the significance of staying at Etzion Gaver for one year unlike all the others?

The identification of the location of the hidden Kadesh holds the key.

- In Numbers 14:25, following the Sin of the Spies, the Israelites are instructed to turn to the wilderness.
- In the next chapter, verse 32, the Torah relates the episode of the *mekoshesh* (gatherer), who profaned the Sabbath in the wilderness by gathering wood. Since the Torah does not specify when this occurred, the straightforward indication is that it took place immediately after the Israelites were exiled to the wilderness, and indeed this is indicated in the *Sifra*.[2]
- Accordingly, this event must have taken place at the first encampment following the Sin of the Spies, which we have determined in chapter 2 was at Kadesh, just east of the tip of the Gulf of Aqaba.

This location is right next to Etzion Gaver, which lies on the tip of the Gulf.

We know that the *mekoshesh* was stoned outside the camp.[3] It would therefore seem likely that the *mekoshesh* was stoned and buried at Etzion Gaver, and this was the cause of the

---

1 At Kadesh from the 2nd year until the 21st year, and at Yotvathah from the 21st year until the 39th year.

2 Leviticus 24:12. See *Sifrei*, Numbers 15:32, and commentary of Rabbeinu Hillel, who reconciles it with *Sifra*.

3 Numbers 15:36.

later encampment and the prolonged stay of one year. Evidently, the Israelites returned here to reinforce their appreciation of the significance of the laws of Sabbath at the very place where the Sabbath had been profaned.[4]

4    It is fascinating to note that the word Etzion (עציון) can be read *eitzin*, which means "wood" and the word Gaver (גבר) means "man." The two words, "gathered together" hints at the sin of the man who gathered the wood at this place.

CHAPTER THIRTEEN

# The Fourth Stage of the Exile: Part I

B y this final stage of the exile, the generation of the spies that was destined to die had already died,[1] although, as we will see later, this was still not known to the Israelites. We will discover that these five last encampments, besides for the unexpected encampment at Hor Hahar, were all final preparations for the Israelites to exit the wilderness.

## Encampment 33
## KADESH (22)

Biblical Reference: **Numbers 33:36, 20:1–13**

Timeline: **40th year from Exodus, Nissan, the 1st month**

Journey: **The Israelites leave Etzion Gaver and travel to Kadesh.**

### Event

Miriam dies on the 10th of Nissan[2] and is buried there. Following her passing, the Israelites complain of a lack of water. Moses and Aaron are instructed by the Almighty to gather the congregation and in front of them bring forth water from a rock. Moses and Aaron gather the people and Moses addresses them, calling them rebels. He then hits the rock twice and water gushes out. Following this event, Moses and Aaron are told that they failed to sanctify the Almighty

---

1    *Tanchuma, Parashas Chukas* 14.

2    *Shulchan Aruch, Orach Chaim* 580:2.

and therefore would not merit to enter into the Holy Land. The commentators try to fathom what exactly was the sin of Moses and Aaron.

## Location

The verse[3] specifies that this Kadesh was also called the wilderness of Tzin. This directs us to the Kadesh where the spies were sent from, 40 years before, which we know from Numbers 13:21 was by the wilderness of Tzin. This Kadesh, as we have learned in chapter 1, was situated at the south-eastern corner of Canaan, by the southwestern corner of the Dead Sea.[4] This indeed is right next to Wadi Tzin, still called by that name today.

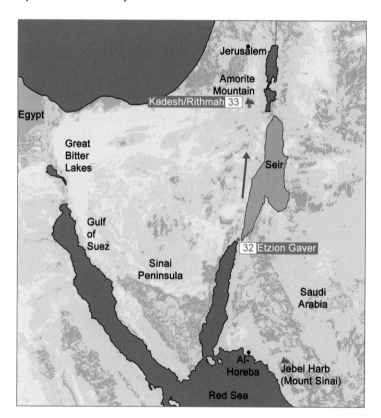

3    Numbers 33:36.
4    Numbers 13:21, 26, and 34:3.

## CHAPTER FOURTEEN

# The Death of Miriam

The identification of the location of the encampment of Kadesh might now serve as a crucial clue for unlocking the mystery surrounding the death of Miriam.

We know that the entire generation of the spies forfeited their right to enter the land of Canaan because of their part in the Sin of the Spies. However, the women did not sin and were not included,[1] and certainly not Miriam the Prophetess, so why did Miriam not merit to enter the Holy Land?

The place where she died might hold the key. We have now established that Miriam died at the very place where the Sin of the Spies took place. Her death at this particular place may be a hint to the cause of her death.

At Hatzeiroth, Miriam spoke out against Moses and, as a result, contracted leprosy. After waiting for her recovery, the Israelites then traveled to Kadesh and sent out the spies. The spies came back and spoke badly of the land.

We are told in *Sotah* 2a that one who sees the consequence of an unfaithful woman should refrain from wine, the cause of the sin. This is because seeing or hearing about a transgression committed can dampen the sense of the severity of the sin and can eventually cause the witness himself to sin.

The spies witnessed the sin of Miriam, and this may have played a part in their own sin of speaking against the Land. Since Miriam was indirectly responsible for this, this may explain why she too was not allowed into the Holy Land.

---

1    *Sifri*, Numbers 26:64.

CHAPTER FIFTEEN

# The Well of Miriam

A glaring question addressed by the Sages is why the Israelites complained for water just after the death of Miriam. How had they managed throughout the 40 years?

The *Beraisa* in *Taanis* 9a deduces from this that the rock that Moses hit was actually the rock he had hit and from which he had brought forth water in Horeb 40 years before. This rock accompanied them from then on throughout their sojourns, but when Miriam died the rock disappeared among the other rocks, revealing that it was in the merit of Miriam that the Israelites had been blessed with this miraculous wellspring. In the merit of Moses and Aaron, it was returned once again.

However, the *Ramban* points out that the straightforward indication of the verse is that there were two separate rocks, and the one in Horeb did not travel with the Israelites in the following encampments. This is also the straightforward indication from Psalms, Isaiah, and another opinion in Rabbinic Tradition:

- The bringing forth of water in the wilderness from a rock is mentioned twice in Psalms[1] and once in Isaiah,[2] and each time the verse makes a double reference with slightly different descriptions. The straightforward indication is that the verse is describing two separate events.
- Indeed, this would explain the opinion of *Midrash Aggadah*, which says that the sin of Moses and Aaron

1    78:15–16, 114:8.
2    48:21.

was that they should have spoken to the rock instead of hitting it, as then the Israelites would have learned a lesson from the rock to listen to the word of the Almighty. If the selfsame rock was the one that was originally hit and used throughout the 40 years, why would Moses have been asked to speak to the rock just now?

- Furthermore, the *Targum* in Psalms 78:15 translates the first reference as splitting open "mountains." This is evidently referring to the event at Horeb.[3] There,[4] the verse opens by referring to *"ha'tzur—*the rock," and says that the Almighty was standing on it. The same word, *ha'tzur*, is also used later, in Exodus 33:21, referring to the mountain itself at Horeb.

Indeed, Jebel Harb, which we have identified as Mount Sinai, takes the form of a gigantic rock, and there is indeed a large crack in the rock behind the head of the mountain, with signs of the bed of a river flowing down from it. This may well have been the crack Moses made when he was told to hit "the rock."[5]

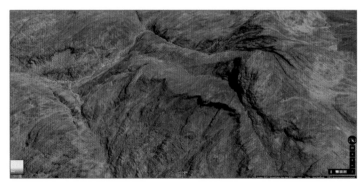

Attribution: Google Earth map data, 2017

## The Song of the Well

According to the above, we can now discern a straightforward interpretation of the Song of the Well referenced in Numbers 21:17. We will see later that the verse is cryptically worded and hints at the praise and adulation sung by the Israelites after their miraculous salvation at Wadi Arnon. However, the verse can now also be interpreted literally to

3   This also explains why the plural form *tzurim* is used here, and the reference to waters coming up from the depths. According to the *Rokeach* (Exodus 19:17), Mount Sinai was in the form of one mountain on top of another. Evidently, the rock was split right through to the bottom of the mountain to allow the waters to come up from the depths.

4   Exodus 17:6.

5   This would now explain the reference to the splitting of the rock in Psalms 78:15 and Isaiah 48:21.

refer to the song and adulation the Israelites sang upon receiving the well at Kadesh, referenced in the previous verse.[6]

## Water Supplies throughout the Forty Years

Following the opinion that there were indeed two separate events of water coming out of stone, we are confronted with the problem of why only at Kadesh was there a need for water and not at all the other encampments throughout the 40 years of wanderings. Our findings in this study can now explain this.

- We have discovered that the Israelites stayed for 19 years in Kadesh next to the tip of the Gulf of Aqaba, and another 19 years in Yotvathah.
- In *Searching for Sinai*, we identified the encampment of Eilim as also being right next to the tip of the Gulf, close to **Eil**ath, **Eil**ot and **Eil** Paran. At Eilim, the Torah informs us that there were twelve wellsprings of water.[7] We have also discovered that Yotvathah is right next to the tip of the Gulf and referred to in the Torah too as a land of flowing waters.
- All the other places following the Sin of the Spies were for very short times, possibly even just one day.
- Traveling to the different places would also not have been problematic. Livnah, Rimon Paretz, and Risah were all within a few days' journey from Kadesh and they would have had enough provisions to last. From Risah, they may have traveled to Keheilathah via Kadesh, where they could refill their water canisters.
- Keheilathah, Har Shafer, Haradah, Makheiloth, Thachath, and Tharach were all close to Mount Sinai, which had the flowing water coming out from the crack in the rock made by Moses.
- The journey from Tharach to Mithkah must have been long, but once again they could refill on the way at Kadesh, and knowing that they were heading to atone for the sin at Marah/Mithkah, just as they had done at Tharach, they would have made sure to add enough provisions for the journey.

6   Pointed out by Rabbi Pesach Bodenheimer.
7   Exodus 15:27.

8    They stayed at Kivroth
     Hataavah one month.
     We have identified
     Kivroth Hataavah
     next to Hatzeiroth
     and Kadesh, based on
     the *Midrash Aggadah*
     that they arrived there
     three days after leaving
     Horeb. This is based
     on the straightforward
     interpretation of the
     verse in Numbers 10:33.
     However, *Midrash
     Aggadah* also gives an
     interpretation according
     to *drash* that could
     imply that they arrived
     there after one day of
     travel. If the encamp-
     ment indeed took place
     according to *drash*—as
     we have found, for
     example, with Marah in
     *Searching for Sinai*—this
     would mean that the
     encampment was 120
     Hebraic miles from
     Horeb. It is fascinating
     to note that this takes
     us to the well at Bir
     el-Hind, which is in
     fact the only well in the
     whole stretch of the
     Saudi Arabian desert.

9    This may have been
     done by the Amalekites
     at the nearby Hormah,
     who may have learned
     via merchants who
     passed by the Israelite
     camp that the exile
     decreed upon them was
     to last only 40 years (see
     *Yoma* 75b). Accordingly,
     they may have tried to
     hamper the oncoming
     journey of the Israelites
     toward Canaan at the
     end of the 40 years.

- At Marah, the water may still have remained sweet and they could have refilled in preparation for their journey to Hashmonah and the neighboring Moseiroth, and they might have topped up as they passed by Nahal Mitzraim/El-Arish.
- From Moseiroth they traveled to B'nei Yaakan, where there were once again wells of water, and the following encampments until Yotvathah were all close at hand.

What remains unaccounted for is Kadesh (as well as the neighboring encampments Hatzeiroth and Kivroth Hataavah[8]), the very place where the Israelites complained for water after the death of Miriam. Forty years before, they sent out the spies from the same place and awaited their return after 40 days. If there was no water there, as the Israelites themselves testified 40 years later, how on earth had they managed to reside there for 40 days?

The answer to this may be hidden in the subtle wording of the Torah.

In Deuteronomy 10:6, mention is made of the time the Israelites traveled to the consecutive encampments B'nei Yaakan, Gudgod, and Yotvathah. The verse refers to the encampment at B'nei Yaakan as "the Wells of B'nei Yaakan," however when listing all the encampments throughout their sojourn in the wilderness, the verse in Numbers 33:32 simply refers to it as B'nei Yaakan.

We can now understand why. Evidently, at the time the Israelites encamped at B'nei Yaakan, which we saw was in the 21st year from the Exodus, there were wells at B'nei Yaakan, but by the end of the 40 years, the wells had either dried up or had been blocked up.[9] Thus, when listing the encampments at the end of the 40 years, the Torah refers to it just as B'nei Yaakan.

In chapter 11, we identified B'nei Yaakan as being next to Hor Hahar/Petra, which is about 90 km from the encampment at Kadesh by the corner of the Dead Sea. Accordingly, while the Israelites waited for the spies' return, they would have been able to replenish their water supplies by sending out dispatchers to the wells of B'nei Yaakan.[10]

## The Rock of Miriam

In line with the above opinion that until the 40th year in the wilderness the Israelites did not have the miraculous well, and it did not disappear at the death of Miriam but was only given to them after her death, we can still understand why this miraculous stone that accompanied the Israelites from Kadesh onward is referred to in Rabbinic Tradition as the "Well of Miriam."

When Moses is instructed about the rock, it is referred to as "**the** rock," with the definite article. If this was the first time the Israelites were introduced to this miraculous stone, it would have been unknown to them and Moses; we would therefore not expect the definite article to be used, which implies the known rock.

The definite article might be there to hint that the rock referred to was a rock that had already been designated for something else at this place. This would then be referring to the rock of the setting stone, that was no doubt, in line with Jewish custom, placed at the cave of Miriam,[11] like we find with Rachel.[12]

10   As we have seen, before the Sin of the Spies the Israelites were traveling at a pace of three times the normal speed; if the dispatchers did the same on the long summer day, they might have even been able to go and return on the same day.

11   It is fascinating to note that by rearranging the letters of the words of the verse in Numbers 20:10, describing what Moses said to the people, "ויאמר להם שמעו נא המרים המן הסלע הזה נוציא לכם מים," we can form the words, "ויאמרו להם השמע נא הנה מסלע מרים הזה נוציא לכם מים," which means "and they said to them, 'Behold, from the rock of Miriam we will bring forth for you water.'"

12   Genesis 35:20. The word in Hebrew for "setting stone" is *matzeivah*, and it is from the same root as the word *vateisatzav*, used to describe Miriam standing firm in wait by the cradle of Moses in Exodus 2:4. This might be hinting that in the merit of Miriam's waiting by the reeds, her *matzeivah* was blessed to provide water for the Israelites.

## CHAPTER SIXTEEN

# The Sin of Mei Merivah

In light of the view expanded on in the previous chapter that the Well of Miriam was only introduced to the Israelites at Kadesh in the 40th year of the exile in the desert, we are now able to gain new insight into the cryptic wording of the episode of Mei Merivah and reveal a new understanding of the sin of Moses and Aaron.

Moses was instructed to take the staff from the Tabernacle and gather the congregation together with Aaron, and that they should "speak to the rock" in front of the congregation and it would bring forth water. The verse repeats that he[1] was to bring forth water from the rock and emphasizes that he was to give the congregation and their animals to drink.

The verse then says that Moses and Aaron gathered the assembly in front of the rock and Moses addressed them saying, "Listen now, rebels. Can we bring water from this rock?" He then struck the rock twice and much water came out, and the congregation and their animals drank. According to *Midrash Aggadah*, the first time he did this, just a few drops came out.[2]

Straight after this episode, the Almighty addresses Moses and Aaron telling them that because they did not believe Him, to sanctify Him in front of the Children of Israel, they forfeited the merit of entering the Holy Land.

This is most puzzling. Where was there a lack of faith? And what did Aaron do? Was not Moses the one who carried out the instructions?

---

1   The verse begins with the plural and then changes to the singular, evidently to imply that Moses was to be acting on behalf of Aaron too.

2   This is deduced from the fact that the verse emphasizes that much water came out after the second time.

Furthermore, if we look back at the instructions given to Moses, we can discern that everything Moses did in front of the assembly he had extrapolated from the instructions.

Moses addressed the rebels based on the instruction to speak to the rock, which he understood to imply that he was to speak *about* the rock, rather than directly *to* the rock.[3] From the instruction to take the staff and bring forth water himself from the rock, Moses understood that he was to hit the rock. Because the instructions referred twice to water coming out the rock, and only after the second time was Moses told to give the congregation and the animals to drink, Moses understood that he was to hit the rock twice, as only a little water would come out the first time.

However, if we take a careful look at the wording of the instruction to gather the congregation, which Aaron was also instructed to be involved in, and then compare this with the wording describing what Moses and Aaron actually did, we find a subtle change. Furthermore, this change seems to be alluded to in the words of the Almighty afterward.

The verse begins by saying that the whole congregation arrived at Kadesh and that after the death of Miriam, there was no water for the congregation. Note that both times, the word used for "congregation" is "*eidah*."

The verse then says that the people complained to Moses about the lack of water. The word used here for "people" is "*am*", which usually denotes the peripheral section of the congregation.[4]

Moses is then told to take the staff and together with Aaron assemble the congregation. Once again, the word used for "the congregation" is "*ha'eidah*."

However, the verse continues to relate that Moses and Aaron assembled the congregation in front of the rock. The word used for "congregation" is "*kahal*." This is the same word used to describe the assembly of rebels that complained about the water in the verses before. The verse continues with Moses addressing this assembly, calling them "rebels."

The indication is that Moses and Aaron only gathered together the ones who complained. "*Eidah*" can refer to just

3  See the *Ramban*, who cites several examples of such terminology.

4  See *Sifri*, Numbers 11:1.

a small part of the congregation,[5] and they evidently understood that this was the interpretation of "*eidah*" referred to in this instruction.[6] But the real intent of the Almighty was to gather the whole congregation, and the verse hints to this by using a different word in describing who Moses and Aaron actually gathered, which indicates that the instruction to assemble the "*eidah*" was not fulfilled.

When the Almighty informs Moses and Aaron that they would not enter the Holy Land, they are told that they would not take "this assembly" into the Land of Canaan. The emphasis is on the wording of "**this** congregation," as opposed to the expected "**the** congregation" (which would imply the whole congregation of Israelites, not just the rebels), as well as the further the usage of the word "*kahal*." This hints that the fault lay both in the makeup of the congregation that was assembled and in the misinterpretation of the word "*Eidah*" given in the instruction to mean the "*kahal*" of the rebels. Since this was the first time the rock of Miriam was introduced to the Israelites, the Almighty wanted the whole congregation to witness the very first time the rock poured forth water after being struck by Moses. Moses and Aaron, being on the high spiritual level that they were, were expected to have understood the real intent of the Almighty. They opted for their own interpretation because they did not believe that the alternative interpretation was actually what the Almighty meant. The sin therefore was not **believing** the Almighty of His true intention.

5    As we find, for example, in Numbers 14:27 and 17:5.

6    While the same word, עדה, was used in the instruction to give the people and their animals to drink, which would surely have included the whole congregation, Moses and Aaron may have thought that even so, the first mention of עדה previously was only referring to the rebels. Alternatively, Moses and Aaron may have thought that the second עדה was also only referring to the rebels. This is because the earlier verse does not mention that the animals were lacking water; only the rebels claimed so. Thus, Moses and Aaron might have understood the instruction to give "the congregation and their animals" to drink to be referring to the rebels, as the rest of the congregation would have just needed water for themselves.

## CHAPTER SEVENTEEN

# Hor Hahar

---
Encampment 34
---

## HOR HAHAR (23)

Biblical Reference: Numbers 33:37, 20:22–21:3

Timeline: 40th year from Exodus, between Nissan and Av, the 1st and 5th months

Journey: The Israelites leave Kadesh and journey to Hor Hahar.

## Event

Aaron dies on the first of the fifth month (Av), is buried there, and Elazar his son is appointed High Priest in his stead. Following Aaron's death, the Clouds of Glory disappear,[1] and the Amalekites[2] on hearing this disguise themselves by speaking in the tongue of Canaanites,[3] and attack, taking a captive. The Israelites, after pledging to give the spoils to the Tabernacle, retaliate and destroy them and fulfill their promise.

## Location

As we saw in chapter 11, we know from Numbers 20:23 that Hor Hahar lay on the border of Edom. Edom, we know was situated on Mount Se'ir[4] and, as we mentioned earlier,[5] is the stretch of mountain that extends from the corner of the Dead Sea down to Eilath and Etzion Gaver by the Gulf of Aqaba on the tip of the eastern arm of the Red Sea, as

---

1   *Rosh Hashanah* 3a.
2   *Midrash Tanchuma* 18.
3   *Midrash Aggadah* (*Rashi*, Numbers 21:1).
4   Genesis 36:9, 16.
5   Chapter 4.

indicated in Deuteronomy 2:8 and Kings I 9:26. The exact location of Hor Hahar is widely identified as Jebel Harun (Mount Aaron) opposite the ancient city of Petra, which is about 80 km south of our location of Kadesh, and slightly to the east. Hor Hahar means "the mountain of the mountain," and *Midrash Tanchuma*[6] explains that it was a mountain on top of a mountain, and indeed Jebel Harun fits this criterion.

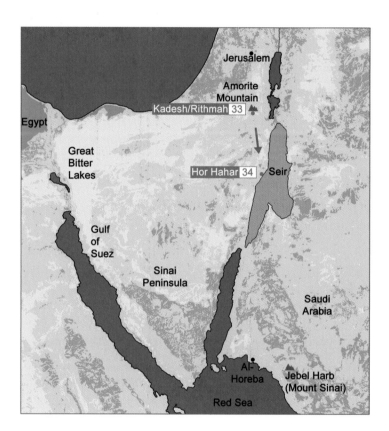

6   Numbers 14.

CHAPTER EIGHTEEN

# Moseiroth (Second Time)

Biblical Reference: Deuteronomy 10:6

Timeline: 40th year from Exodus, Av, the 5th month

Journey: After the trauma of Aaron's passing, the Israelites leave Hor Hahar and head back toward Egypt and arrive at Moseiroth once again. This journey was not initiated by Divine instruction and therefore this encampment is not listed in the travels of the Israelites in Numbers 33, and does not comprise one of the 42 encampments.

## Event

The Levites chase after them to bring them back. At Moseiroth, a fight ensues and seven families of the Israelites fall, one from the tribe of Shimon, one from the tribe of Gad, and five from the tribe of Benjamin. The Levites also lose four families.[1] The Clouds of Glory return in the merit of Moses.[2]

## Explanation

- As we saw in chapter 11, after leaving Moseiroth, the Israelites traveled to B'nei Yaakan.
- However, intriguingly, in Deuteronomy 10:6, the verse says the opposite, that the Israelites traveled from B'nei Yaakan to Moseiroth.
- The *Midrash Tanchuma*[3] explains that indeed the Israelites traveled from Moseiroth to B'nei Yaakan, but

1 Jerusalem Talmud, *Yoma* 2b (*Rashi*, Numbers 26:13).

2 Babylonian Talmud, *Taanis* 9a.

3 Numbers, *Parashas Chukas* 18.

they also traveled from B'nei Yaakan to Moseiroth—at the time that Aaron died.

- When Aaron died, the Clouds of Glory that had led them throughout their travels disappeared. Out of exasperation, the Israelites headed back toward Egypt and arrived at Moseiroth, the seventh encampment before Hor Hahar, the place where Aaron died.[4]

This now can be qualified. We saw in chapter 11 that B'nei Yaakan is in the same area as Hor Hahar. The verse in Deuteronomy 10:6 is telling us that at the time of the death of Aaron, the Israelites traveled from B'nei Yaakan, i.e., Hor Hahar, to Moseiroth heading toward Egypt. Indeed, as can be seen from our maps in chapter 11, this would be the direction to go to get to Egypt, heading north following the outskirts of the populated lands rather than cutting across the wilderness.

## Derech Ha'asarim

With this, we can further understand an obscure verse according to its literal interpretation adopted by *Midrash Aggadah*.

After the death of Aaron, the verse in Numbers 21:1 relates that the Canaanite king of the south heard that the Israelites came *"derech ha'asarim,"* and waged war against them. The words *derech ha'asarim* mean literally "the path of the spies."[5]

This can now be understood to be referring to the Israelites who left Hor Hahar and traveled to Moseiroth. The fact that only a minority of families fell, and that the Levites managed to overpower the Israelites, indicates that the battle involved only a minority of the congregation and was most probably because only a small group of Israelites actually fled from Hor Hahar. The Canaanite king heard about this group going northward to Moseiroth, which as we have seen, was actually another name for Hatzeiroth. Being a small group, and further, taking the same path as the Israelites did 38 years before when they sent out the spies, they believed that these were also spies sent out to spy the land before their oncoming invasion.

4   *Rashi* explains that they literally went back seven encampments, and the Torah in Deuteronomy 10:6—which mentions the death of Aaron and their journey from B'nei Yaakan to Moseiroth—just mentions the last leg of that journey. However, in light of what we have discovered in the previous chapters, going through the seven encampments before Hor Hahar is not a straight route back to Egypt.

5   See commentary of Rabbi Samson Raphael Hirsch.

## Location

We have already identified Moseiroth/Hatzeiroth as being on the southwestern corner of the Dead Sea.

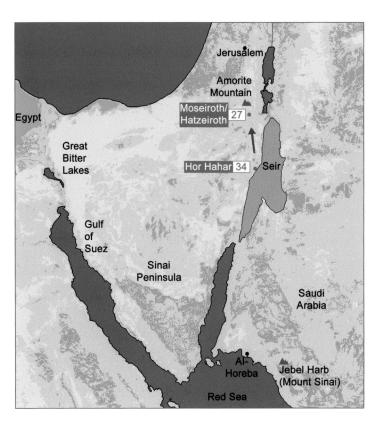

# CHAPTER NINETEEN

# Hormah

We find in the Torah two places called Hormah.

- In Deuteronomy 1:44, Moses relates that following the Sin of the Spies and the decree of wanderings—and despite his warning that it would be futile to attempt to enter Canaan then—a band of Israelites nonetheless attempted to enter Canaan as originally planned via the Amorite mountain. However, they were attacked by the Amalekites and Canaanites from the south who pursued them and killed them at "Se'ir until **Hormah**."

- Another place called Hormah is mentioned in Numbers 21:3. After Aaron died at Hor Hahar, the Canaanite king of Arad from the south attacked the Israelites and took captive a maidservant. The Israelites, after pledging the spoils to the Tabernacle service, retaliated, destroyed them, and then took their cities' spoils and gave them over to the Tabernacle. The place was then called Hormah, because in Hebrew this can mean "destruction" and also "possessions given over to the Tabernacle."

- In light of our discoveries, we can now pinpoint the two Hormahs, and this leads to the fascinating revelation that they both appear to lie in the same area, suggesting very strongly, that they are, in fact, one and the same. This in turn adds further insight to the events that took place there.

- We know that Se'ir is the stretch of mountain from the southeastern corner of the Dead Sea going south until the tip of the Red Sea at Aqaba. Evidently, the verse in Deuteronomy above that says the Israelites were killed "at Se'ir until Hormah" means that they began to be caught as they fled southward along the western border of Se'ir and the last of them got no further than Hormah.
- In chapter 18 we identified Hor Hahar as being opposite the ancient city of Petra, which is next to Se'ir and about 80 km south from the Dead Sea. Numbers 21:2 indicates that the retaliation took place then and there, and verse 3 indicates that the cities destroyed were by the battlefield, next to Hor Hahar. Although the verse refers to the King of Arad, evidently, he had cities outside Canaan on the outskirts of Se'ir at Hormah too.

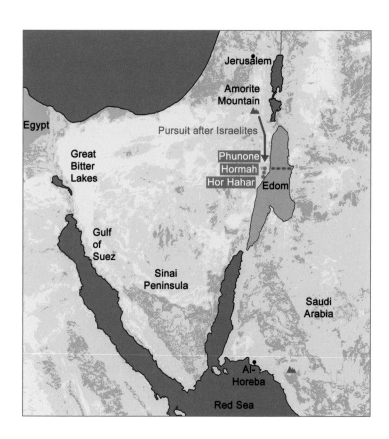

Bearing in mind that the Hormah nearby Hor Hahar was in the flight path of the fleeing Israelites at the time of the Sin of the Spies, then rather than saying that there just happened to be another Hormah along that same path, the natural assumption is that the two Hormahs were actually one and the same.

Indeed, this seems to be hinted at in Numbers 21:3. The text also describes the pursuit of the Israelites from the Amorite mountain by the Amalekites and the killing of the Israelites "until **the** Hormah." Why is the definite article used in describing Hormah? This can now be resolved. The word "HaHormah" in this context is not referring to the name of the place but means "the destruction," i.e., the Israelites were pursued until they were destroyed. The verse does not refer to the name Hormah in Numbers because it was only given that name later, after Aaron died and the Canaanites were destroyed by the Israelites.

Now we can go one step further. *Midrash Aggadah* says that among the Canaanites who attacked the Israelites after the death of Aaron were Amalekites, hinted at by the words "dwellers of the south." Indeed, this would explain why they had cities at Hormah by Se'ir, because the Amalekites were descendants of Edom.[1] Evidently, they were the same Canaanites and Amalekites who lived together in the south at the time of the spies, and pursued the Israelites to their deaths at the Amalekite cities in Hormah.[2]

With this, we can now offer another literal explanation[3] to the obscure verse in Numbers 21:1.

- As we saw in the previous chapter, the verse relates that the attack of the Canaanites after the death of Aaron was instigated after the Canaanite king heard that the Israelites came along "the path of the spies."[4]
- This can now be understood as referring to the band of Israelites that ascended the Amorite mountain despite Moses warning them not to. The Canaanites, who saw just a small group and not the whole army, would have naturally thought that they were a squad of spies sent to check out the land.

---

1 Genesis 36:12.

2 Although they are referred to as living on the mountain (Numbers 14:45), they are also referred to as living in the valley (ibid., 14:25).

3 We have already seen one explanation in the previous chapter.

4 Rabbi Samson Raphael Hirsch. See next chapter for its interpretation according to *drash*.

- The route this band took after fleeing from the Amorite mountain to Hormah on the outskirts of Se'ir was basically the same route that the Israelites took from Kadesh Barnea next to the Amorite mountain, until Hor Hahar.

The verse may be saying that this time (after the death of Aaron), when the Canaanites/Amalekites saw the Israelites taking the same route as the "spies"—which had previously resulted in misfortune—they believed that this path was destined for ill-fortune for the Israelites. They therefore assumed that now would be a prime opportunity to attack and destroy the Israelites, but they were wrong; their attack instead brought about their own destruction.

The name Hormah now has an additional twist. It was not only a commemoration of the destruction of the cities that attacked the Israelites after Aaron died, but also of the vengeance wrought upon the people that had destroyed the Israelites 38 years earlier, in the very same place.

## CHAPTER TWENTY

# The Flattening
# of the Mountains

In *Beraisa D'Meleches Hamishkan*,[1] we are told that the **Clouds of Glory** flattened the hills and mountains and raised the valleys in front of the path of the Israelites through the wilderness. The flattening of the mountains and hills is also referred to in *Berachos* 54b, which relates the miracle that occurred when the Israelites passed through Wadi Arnon. However, there we are told that this was done by the **Ark of the Covenant**. An enigmatic verse in Deuteronomy now allows us to reconcile these two traditions.

In Deuteronomy 10, Moses recalls that after the smashing of the first Tablets of stone, he was instructed to hew out a second set of Tablets and put them into an Ark made of wood. The verse then continues, seemingly digressing, by mentioning the death of Aaron at B'nei Yaakan. In chapter 11, we discovered that B'nei Yaakan was one and the same as Hor Hahar, the place recorded in Numbers 20 for the death of Aaron, but why mention the death of Aaron at this point?

- In Jerusalem Talmud, *Sotah*,[2] we are told that there were actually two Arks: one made by Betzalel for the Tabernacle, and this housed the second Tablets of stone, and one made by Moses, mentioned here in Deuteronomy, which housed the broken Tablets.[3]
- The Jerusalem Talmud also says that the Ark of Moses was the Ark mentioned in Numbers 10:33, which

1    Chapter 14.

2    35a.

3    Although the verse in Deuteronomy 10 says that Moses put the second Tablets in **his** Ark, evidently, they were only put there temporarily until Moses returned after the second set of 40 days that he spent at the top of the mountain learning the Torah again after the Sin of the Golden Calf.

traveled a path of three days ahead of the Israelites to prepare the way for them.

- *Taanis* 9a tells us that when Aaron died, the Clouds of Glory that existed in his merit disappeared, but they later returned in the merit of Moses.

We are now in a position to explain the verse in Deuteronomy 10 and at the same time reconcile the apparently conflicting traditions as to what flattened the mountains.

The mountains and hills were initially flattened by the Clouds of Glory that passed in front of the Israelites, which they received at Succoth just after they left Egypt, and continued to occur throughout the 40 years in the wilderness. However, when Aaron died and the Clouds of Glory disappeared, the duty was then given over to the Ark of Moses.[4] The verse in Deuteronomy 10 therefore alludes to the death of Aaron while relating about the Ark of Moses in order to imply that his death had relevance to the Ark of Moses due to the duty given over to it at this time.

## Derech Ha'asarim

With this, we can further understand the obscure verse mentioned in the last two chapters, this time according to its midrashic interpretation.

As we mentioned above in chapter 18, after the death of Aaron, the verse in Numbers 21:1 relates that the Canaanite king of the south heard that the Israelites came *"derech ha'asarim"* and waged war against them. The words *derech ha'asarim* literally mean "the path of the spies." However, *Midrash Tanchuma* 18, following an explanation according to *drash*, interprets it to mean "the path of the great navigator," referring to the Ark of the Covenant that went before the Israelites to show them the way. This is difficult to understand, as at this point in time, as we saw in chapter 17, the Israelites were not heading toward Canaan but rather in the opposite direction. Furthermore, what is the significance of being navigated by the Ark of the Covenant?

This can now be understood.

4   Although the Clouds of Glory returned, the duty was not taken away from the Ark of Moses in the same way that it was not taken away from the Clouds of Glory when Moses made the Ark.

Up until the death of Aaron, the Clouds of Glory flattened the mountains and hills in front of the path of the Israelites, but following his death, the task was taken over by the Ark of the Covenant; this is what the verse is referring to when it describes the Israelites "coming along the path" of the Great Navigator.[5] In doing so, the verse means to allude to the death of Aaron, which caused the Clouds of Glory to disappear, and to point out that it was Aaron's death that instigated the attack. After losing the merit of the righteous Aaron, the Canaanites thought they might now succeed in destroying the Israelites.

This also explains the verse in Numbers 33:40:

- In the middle of summarizing the sojourns throughout the 40 years of wandering, the verse intriguingly relates that following the death of Aaron, the Canaanite king in the south heard about something, "with the coming of the Israelites."
- Even more surprisingly, the verse stops there and does not elaborate further.

We can now understand that the verse means that the Canaanite king heard something with regard to the coming of the Israelites. The verse does not mean to dwell on what happened afterward in the same way it does not dwell on what happened at all the other encampments. It mentions solely the news received by the Canaanite king because it has relevance to the nature of the sojourns from that point onward with regard to who flattened the path in front of the Israelites. What the Canaanite king heard about was the disappearance of the Clouds of Glory that flattened the mountains in front of the coming Israelites.[6] This is what the verse means "with regard to the coming of the Israelites."[7]

5   The Canaanites might have learned about Aaron's death by observing that the Ark went ahead of the Israelites alone without the Clouds of Glory as they prepared to leave Hor Hahar.

6   *Rosh Hashanah* 3a.

7   According to the literal explanation adopted by *Midrash Aggadah* mentioned in chapter 18, "Derech Ha'asarim," the verse can be explained here to hint at the unauthorized journey of the Israelites towards Moseiroth. It was this coming of the Israelites that the Canaanite king heard.

# The Second Hidden Journey to Kadesh

Biblical Reference: Numbers 20:14–21, 21:4–9,
Deuteronomy 2:1–8

Timeline: 40th year from Exodus, Av, the 5th month

Journey: The Israelites leave Moseiroth and travel
to Kadesh.

In chapter 2, we discovered hidden between the verses an additional journey of the Israelites to a concealed Kadesh, at the beginning of the exile in the wilderness, just after the Sin of the Spies. This Kadesh was situated on the corner of Se'ir next to the tip of the Gulf of Aqaba. Further analysis of the verses now reveals another hidden journey to the selfsame Kadesh, at the end of the exile.

- In Numbers 20:1, the verse relates the Israelite arrival in the wilderness of Tzin (in the 40th year), that they stayed in Kadesh, and that Miriam died there.
- In Numbers 20:14, the verse says that the Israelites sent out messengers from Kadesh to the King of Edom telling him that the Israelites were residing at the corner of Edom and sought permission to pass through his land (in order to go into the land of Canaan).
- The simple understanding of these verses is that the messengers were sent out from the **same Kadesh**.
- But this could not have been so, because the Kadesh of the wilderness of Tzin lay on the northwestern

corner of Mount Se'ir, on the southeastern corner of Canaan[1] by the Dead Sea, and the Israelites would not have needed to pass through Edom from there to get to Canaan. On the contrary, this would be going in the opposite direction.

- Furthermore, Judges 11:16,18 indicates that the messengers were sent out from a different Kadesh at the southwestern corner of Se'ir next to the Red Sea.[2]

## Location

We have already identified this Kadesh in chapter 2 as being located next to the tip of the Gulf of Aqaba.

## Order of Journeys

Numbers 20:15–21 continues to relate about the request to pass through Edom, and the subsequent refusal of the Edomites, and in verse 22, it says that the Israelites left Kadesh and came to Hor Hahar. The simple indication is that

1  As indicated in Numbers 13:21 and 33:36. We now know that the wilderness was so called because it is next to the Wadi Tzin, still called by that name today.

2  This might actually be hinted to in Numbers 20:1. The verse mentions first that they arrived in the wilderness of Tzin and then says that they stayed in Kadesh. The straightforward meaning is that the verse mentions the region, i.e., the wilderness of Tzin, and then specifies Kadesh where they stayed within the region of the wilderness of Tzin. However, we can now discern that the verse in Numbers 20:1 may actually be referencing two encampments: "the wilderness of Tzin," i.e., the Kadesh by the Dead Sea; and later on "they stayed at Kadesh" on the southwestern corner of Se'ir, which the verse dwells upon later in verse 14. This may be why *Targum Yonasan* does not translate the words "they stayed in Kadesh," in order to hint that they are not related to the central issue of the verse.

the Israelites must have traveled to the southern Kadesh after leaving the northern Kadesh, and following Edom's refusal to let them pass through, they then traveled to Hor Hahar. However, from a number of different pointers, it appears that the journey to the southern Kadesh and the request to enter Edom actually occurred **after** they left Hor Hahar.

- First, if they were destined to go to Hor Hahar, why would they first ask Edom if they could pass through their land?

- Second, in Deuteronomy 2:3, Moses is told by the Almighty that they had encircled Se'ir long enough and they should now turn northward. The straight-forward implication is that this took place at the southern Kadesh, and this is what instigated the request to Edom to pass through their land.

- However, if they were in Kadesh before going to Hor Hahar, then we have the problem that the Israelites at this point were still destined to encircle Se'ir **one more time** after they returned from Hor Hahar.

- Furthermore, why does verse 8 follow by saying that they came down the Aravah, passing Eilath and Etzion Gaver, when in fact they headed in the opposite direction toward Hor Hahar?[3]

- Finally, if the Israelites traveled to the southern Kadesh before journeying to Hor Hahar, the sum total of encampments will be 43, but we know from chapter 2 that there were only 42 encampments. We will see in the next chapter that given that the journey to the southern Kadesh was after Hor Hahar, this can be reconciled.

Evidently then, the Israelites traveled from the northern Kadesh **straight to** Hor Hahar and only **after** the encampment of Hor Hahar did they travel to the southern Kadesh and request passageway from Edom. After they were refused, they then headed north down the Aravah from Eilath and Etzion Gaver (which was right next to Kadesh[4]) to go away from Edom.

3    It can't mean the opposite, that they went north along the Aravah from Eilath and Etzion Gaver to get to Hor Hahar, because the verse says that they went away from the Edomites in Se'ir—but Hor Hahar was right next to Se'ir.

4    This now explains why Etzion Gaver is mentioned although it is right next to Eilath. The verse does not mean to point out places they passed, only the place they set out from, which was Kadesh Barnea, right next to Eilath and Etzion Gaver.

In Numbers 21:4, the verse says that the Israelites traveled from Hor Hahar toward the Red Sea in order go around Se'ir. This is referring to the journey to Kadesh with the intent to encircle the southwestern corner of Edom and enter Edom from the south. Indeed, this would be the first place to request from Edom to pass through their land, as there is a direct path from there cutting through Se'ir[5] that would have led them to the straits of Moab where they finally encamped before crossing into Canaan.

In Numbers 21:4, the verse says that the Israelites left Hor Hahar and were troubled because of the journey. They spoke against the Almighty and Moses and disparagingly about the manna. This can now be understood as having been instigated by the letdown they experienced at Kadesh after hearing Edom's refusal to allow them to pass through their land.[6]

The Torah, in Numbers 20:22–29, by mentioning the journey from Kadesh to Hor Hahar **after** relating the request to Edom at the southern Kadesh, is concealing that this journey was from a different Kadesh than the one mentioned just before where Miriam died. It also effectively conceals the journey from Hor Hahar to the Kadesh on the southwest corner of Se'ir, just as it did with the journey to this selfsame Kadesh 38 years before. Why the Torah does so will be discussed in the next chapter.

### Event

Moses sends messengers to the king of Edom asking permission for the Israelites to pass through his land, but Edom refuses.

### Where Were They Heading?

In their initial journey toward the land of Canaan before the Sin of the Spies, the Israelites headed to the southern border of Canaan in order to enter from the south. However, following the 40 years of wandering, the Israelites came around to the eastern border of Canaan and encamped by the Jordan River, then entered from the east. It was in order to get to the east side of Canaan that they requested from Edom to pass through their land.

5    On the western border from Hor Hahar there would be no entry into Se'ir, due to the steep incline.

6    Pointed out by Rabbi Pesach Bodenheimer.

Why they did not take the same route as before can be explained by the verse in Deuteronomy 1:8, as pointed out by Rabbi Pesach Bodenheimer. The verse says that in their initial journey they were instructed to enter the land and inherit it. The *Sifri* deduces from the verse that they would have received the land without raising a sword, as the Canaanites and the neighboring nations would have submitted their lands to them without fighting. Accordingly, they could have taken the straight route through the southern border of Canaan.

However, following the Sin of the Spies, the Israelites lost this luxury and were required to take the land by force. The natural way of conquering was then first to neutralize Sichon on the other side of the Jordan, who was paid by the Canaanites to protect them.[7]

7   *Midrash Tanchuma, Parashas Chukas* 23.

## CHAPTER TWENTY-TWO

# The Graves of the Six Hundred Thousand

After the Sin of the Spies, it was decreed upon the whole generation of six hundred thousand Israelites who came out of Egypt that they were to die, although not all at once, over a period of 40 years, during which they would wander through the wilderness.[1] *Midrash Eichah* says that their deaths were spread out over the 40 years, however they only died one day a year, on the 9th of Av, which was the day of the sin.

The natural assumption is that their graves must have been spread out across the wilderness, at the sites of the various encampments, but we can now deduce that they were actually all buried in the same place!

- We have discovered that for the first 19 years, the Israelites resided in Kadesh, and the last 18 years they stayed in Yotvathah, which is right next to Kadesh, so evidently the vast majority must have all been buried close to each other.
- Furthermore, the verse in Numbers says that the Israelites were to die in the very wilderness that the spies were sent from, and that was the wilderness of Paran, which does not lie in Saudia Arabia.
- We know that all the other encampments took place in the same year, so evidently the Sinai and Saudi Arabian encampments all took place either before or after the 9th of Av of that year, allowing for those

---

1    Numbers 14:26–38.

who died in that year also to be in close proximity to Kadesh.

## The Trek to Kadesh from Hor Hahar

In chapter 24, we will discover that following the death of Aaron, the exile was effectively over. Accordingly, the expected plan would have been to head toward the land of Canaan. Yet we find that from Hor Hahar, the Israelites traveled in the opposite direction, down south to Kadesh at the southwestern corner of Se'ir. We can now understand why. Aaron died on the 1st of Av. Although the bulk of the Israelites were ready to enter Canaan, there were still among them the last of the generation of the spies who were destined to die on 9th of Av. Therefore, the Israelites naturally headed south in order to accompany them to their graves at Kadesh.[2]

## Why Was Kadesh Concealed?

With this, we can also perhaps explain why the Torah persistently disguises the encampment and, indeed, the very existence of the Kadesh Barnea at the southwestern corner of Edom.

- In Deuteronomy 1, Moses describes the arrival at Kadesh at the northwestern corner of Edom on the southeastern corner of Canaan, and the request to send out spies, and the tragic consequences that followed. Moses relates that following the decree of exile, they stayed in Kadesh for 19 years.

- The simple indication of the verse is that Moses is referring to the same Kadesh. However, as we saw in chapter 2, it must have been a different Kadesh, because from Numbers 14:25[3] we see that they left Kadesh Barnea the very next day. So why does the Torah conceal this?

- Furthermore, Moses begins by saying that the journey to Kadesh Barnea was eleven days, and the simple indication is that he is referring to the Kadesh Barnea at the corner of Canaan, but the *Rambam*[4]

2  We will see later in chapter 24 that in fact these people did not die then; they were atoned for instead by the fear of thinking they were going to die.

3  See also Deuteronomy 2:14.

4  *Moreh Nevuchim* 3:50.

says he was actually referring to the Kadesh Barnea at the southwestern corner of Edom. We have indeed found remarkable mathematical corroboration to this, mentioned earlier in chapter 4, so once again, why is this concealed?

- Furthermore, we find that at the end of the 40 years the Israelites encamped a second time at the Kadesh on the southwestern corner of Edom, yet once again this is also concealed. In Numbers 20, the Torah relates the encampment at Kadesh and the death of Miriam at the end of the 40 years, and then in verse 14, of the request from Kadesh to the King of Edom to pass through his land in order to enter Canaan. The simple indication is that the verse is talking about the same Kadesh. However, on further inspection, as we saw in the previous chapter, this is surely not so, because the Kadesh in verse 1 was the wilderness of Tzin, which is on the southwestern corner of Canaan. From there they would not have needed to pass through the land of Edom in order to enter Canaan, and on the contrary, to do so would have meant going in the opposite direction. Therefore, they must have been at the other Kadesh on the southwest corner of Edom, yet the Torah conceals this too.[5]

We can now understand this because, evidently, the six hundred thousand were buried in Kadesh, and if this were to have become common knowledge, the grounds would no doubt have become prey for undesired intruders and curiosity seekers by the masses throughout history,[6] and the gravesite would very likely be profaned. Thus, the site was concealed and the reference of the 19-year encampment at Kadesh was subtly inserted alongside the mention of the Kadesh by the southeastern corner of Canaan in Deuteronomy 1. The same was done with regard to the second time they encamped there, in Numbers 20, so that it would not be readily discerned as a different place.[7]

5    In chapter 21, we saw further that the Torah goes to even further lengths to conceal this encampment by swapping the order of events, mentioning the journey to Hor Hahar after the request from Edom.

6    This is especially so, as *Pirkei D'Rabi Eliezer* (41) says that after witnessing the revelation at Mount Sinai, their bodies did not decompose after death, and no doubt this would have drawn the masses to take a look at this wonder.

7    However, as Rabbi Pesach Bodenheimer points out, the fact that the Torah does not conceal it altogether indicates that it is there to be revealed, and the time to reveal it is evidently now in our generation when we have available the detailed mapping that allows for the insight into the verses.

## The Hidden Rebuke

We can now further attempt to fathom what might be the most obscure verse in the whole Torah.

- Deuteronomy begins with Moses's rebuke to the Israelites at the end of the 40 years of exile on the other side of the Jordan River, but then verse 1 suddenly seems to divert, referencing the wilderness in the Aravah, opposite the Red Sea, between Paran and Tofel and Lavan and Hatzeiroth and Di Zahav.

- The next verse seems to divert again without explanation, referencing an 11-day journey from Horeb toward Mount Se'ir until Kadesh Barnea.[8]

- The following verse then goes back to relate at length what Moses said to the Israelites in the land of Moab just before he died.

A literal explanation can now be discerned. The verse is actually concealing another rebuke made by Moses "on the other side of the Jordan River." The Jordan River comes down from the north and spills into the Dead Sea, but it actually continues, evidently underground, and flows from east to west until the Mediterranean Sea.[9] The verse is actually referring to two separate speeches at two different times and two different places. From verse 3 onward, it is referring to what Moses said to the Israelites in the land of Moab to the east of the Jordan River, at the end of the 40 years of exile. The first two verses are referring to what he said south of the Jordan River, at the beginning of the exile, in Kadesh Barnea at the southwestern corner of Edom.

The verse first identifies the location of Kadesh Barnea by saying that it was on the other side of the Jordan, in the desert as well as the Aravah, and situated opposite (to the west) the arm of the Red Sea that lies between the wilderness of Paran and the wilderness of Tofel,[10] and (that this Kadesh Barnea) is situated opposite Lavan (in the east),[11] opposite Hatzeiroth (in the north) and opposite Di Zahav (in the south).[12]

What Moses said there was verse 2, that when they left Horeb heading toward the Amorite mountain, it would

8    See *Rashi* for explanations according to *drash*.

9    *Bava Basra* 55a.

10   Tofel may be a concealed reference to Sin, Dofkah, and Horeb, places where the Israelites encamped in that wilderness (see *Searching for Sinai*) and together (סן דפק וחרב) have the same numerical value as Tofel (תפל). It is fascinating to note that Se'ir (שעיר) is opposite Tofel and has the numerical value of the words מל תפל, which means "opposite Tofel."

11   Lavan means "white," and this might be hinting at the place where they received the manna, which was white (Exodus 16:31) and may have been east of Kadesh Barnea (see *Searching for Sinai*).

12   *Berachos* 32a says this is hinting at the sin of the Golden Calf, which was caused by the great wealth with which they came out from Egypt and the Red Sea (so much so that they exclaimed, "Enough gold—די זהב"). Indeed, the sin of the Golden Calf took place at Horeb, which lies opposite Hatzeiroth in the north, and Kadesh Barnea lies between the two.

normally have taken them 11 days until they crossed the Arabian desert and arrived at Kadesh Barnea. With this, Moses meant for them to reflect upon what they had done. He reminded them of the miracle that the journey took much less time, as hinted at in Numbers 10:33 and qualified by *Sifri*, in order to bring them quicker to the Holy Land.[13] And now, as a result of their sin, they had to remain in the wilderness for 40 years![14]

Once again, this event at Kadesh Barnea is also concealed from the naked eye in order to protect intrusion of the site by the masses in the course of the thousands of years to follow.

13    The Israelites arrived at Sinai on the 1st of the 3rd month, and the Torah specifies that they left Mount Sinai on the 20th of the 2nd month, possibly to point out that those 11 days would have been fitting to stay at Mount Sinai in order to culminate a complete year at Sinai (like we find in Deuteronomy 24:5 and *Sotah* 43a), but the Almighty wanted to usher in their entry to the Holy Land.

14    See *Sifri* on this verse.

CHAPTER TWENTY-THREE

# The Fourth Stage of the Exile, Part II

―――――――― Encampment 35 ――――――――
## TZALMONAH (24)

Biblical Reference: Numbers 33:41, 21:6–9

Timeline: 40th year from Exodus, Av, the 5th month

Journey: The Israelites leave Hor Hahar and travel to Tzalmonah.

## Event

The Israelites, following the refusal of Edom to allow them passage, are exasperated and speak against the Almighty and Moses, complaining that they were taken out of Egypt and speaking disparagingly about the manna.

## Location

We saw in the last two chapters that from Hor Hahar, the Israelites first traveled to Moseiroth and then to the southern Kadesh. Although the journey to Moseiroth was unauthorized, the following journey to Kadesh was. This would make the sum total of official encampments 43, but we have learned in chapter 2 that there were only 42 encampments. However, if Tzalmonah was one and the same as Kadesh, then indeed the number would remain at 42, and this is further corroborated by *Targum Yonasan*.

*Targum Yonasan*[1] says that the exasperation of the Israelites and the disparaging comments about the manna in Numbers 21:5 took place in Tzalmonah. Indeed, the word צלמונה (Tzalmonah) is an anagram of the words לץ המן, which means "mockery of the manna." We deduced in the previous chapter that this was sparked by the disappointment following Edom's refusal to allow them passageway, and indeed this would naturally have taken place there and then at Kadesh.

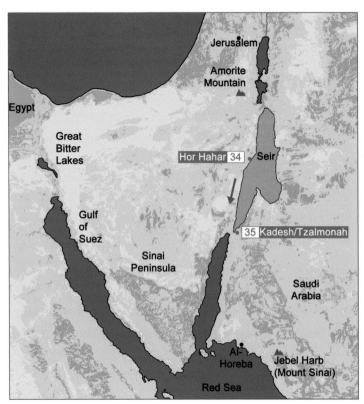

1  Numbers 33:41.
2  *Targum Yonasan*, Numbers 21:6. This is also implicit from verse 10, which relates the journey to Ovoth after describing the episode of the snakes, and in Numbers 33:43, Ovoth is recorded as the encampment after Phunone.
3  3:8.

——————————— Encampment 36 ———————————
# PHUNONE (25)

Biblical Reference: Numbers: 33:42, 21:6–9, Deuteronomy 2:2–8

Timeline: 40th year from Exodus, Av, the 5th month

Journey: The Israelites leave Tzalmonah and travel to Phunone.

## Event

Serpents appear and attack the people, killing many. Moses is instructed to make a serpent of copper and raise it on a banner, and those inflicted by the snakes look toward the copper snake and are healed.[2] The Mishnah in *Rosh Hashanah* qualifies that by looking upward toward the heavens, the inflicted were aroused to repent, and this brought about their recovery.[3]

## Location

In Deuteronomy 2:3, Moses is told that they had encircled Mount Se'ir enough and should now **turn** northward. Moses is also told to peacefully buy food and water from the Edomites along the way. These instructions were evidently said at the southwestern corner of Se'ir, at Kadesh, and accordingly instigated the request to Edom to allow them passageway. The Edomites, however, refused and the Israelites had to go north along the Aravah on the western border of Edom.[4]

If we follow along the Aravah, going north along the western border of Edom, we do indeed arrive at an ancient city called Phainon, just north of the Wadi Faidan.

## Further Event

Judges 11:17 relates that the Israelites requested from Moab as well as Edom to pass through their land, but Moab also refused, and so they had to encircle the land of Moab, coming around to Moab's eastern border.

- Evidently, they journeyed to Phunone with the intent to then head due north through Moab until the straits of Moab next to the Jordan River. However, after Moab refused, they had to head east in order to encircle the land of Moab.
- The verse in Deuteronomy 2:8 says that after going north along the Aravah, they then turned and passed toward the wilderness of Moab.
- The verse implies that at the point they turned they immediately headed toward the wilderness of Moab.[5]
- In the next section, we will see that the encampment

4    2:8. This follows the straightforward indication that verse 8 was a fulfillment of the instruction of verse 3 to head north. *Rashi*, however, in Deuteronomy 2:1 and Numbers 34:3, implies that the Israelites actually headed east along the southern border of Se'ir from here, and not north along the Aravah. He explains the instruction in verse 2 to turn to the north to mean after encircling the southern border of Edom and Moab, and evidently explains verse 8 to refer to the journey from Hor Hahar. However, we find the ancient city of Phainon, along the Aravah, indeed in line with the straightforward indication of the verse. Furthermore, contrary to *Rashi*'s interpretation, archeological discoveries indicate that ancient Moab did not extend as far south as the southern border of Edom, rather over 150 km further north (*Shalosh Artzos L'Shevi'is* [2014], p. 68). Evidently, *Rashi* was prompted to his interpretation because of a question we will address at the end of chapter 24.

5    This is the straightforward implication of the words and the clear indication of the musical notes passed down by Rabbinic Tradition.

of Ovoth was after they headed toward the wilderness of Moab.

- They therefore must have sent out messengers to Moab at the encampment before, i.e., Phunone.[6]
- Indeed, the word פונון (Phunone) is an anagram of the word ונפן, which means "and we turned." This is the word used to describe their journey from this point in Deuteronomy 2:8.

This information will aid us in locating the coming encampments.

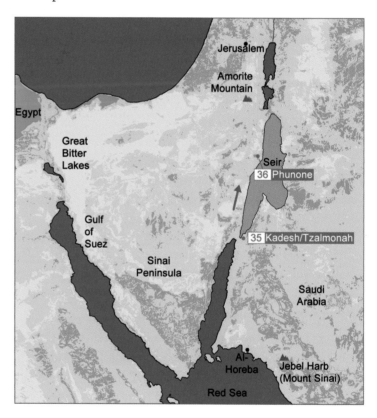

─────── Encampment 37 ───────
## OVOTH (26)

Biblical Reference: Numbers 33:43

Timeline: 40th year from Exodus, Av, the 5th month

Journey: The Israelites leave Phunone and travel to Ovoth.

6   After relating the request to Moab (Judges 11:17), the verse mentions that they stayed in Kadesh. This seems superfluous since it already mentioned Kadesh in verse 16. This can now be explained, as the Kadesh in verse 16 is referring to the southern Kadesh, the place where they sent messengers to Edom, while this Kadesh may be referring to the northern Kadesh, which we know was actually the wilderness of Tzin. Indeed, Phunone is just on the eastern edge of what might also be included as the wilderness of Tzin.

## Event

The Israelites encamp on the southwestern border of Moab and are told not to incite the Moabites to war.

## Location

Between Kadesh/Tzalmonah and Iyei Ha'avarim there were two encampments: Phunone and Ovoth.

- In Numbers 21:11, we are told that the Israelites left Ovoth and journeyed to the wilderness of Moab (on its eastern border).
- In Deuteronomy 2:8, Moses relates that after heading north (to Phunone) they then turned toward the wilderness of Moab. Therefore, Ovoth must evidently have lay on a straight line between Phunone and the wilderness of Moab on its eastern border.
- In the next section, we will see that the encampment at the wilderness of Moab, Iyei Ha'avarim was due east from Phunone.

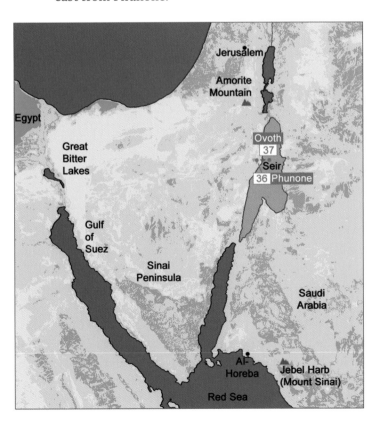

It therefore follows that Ovoth was also due east of Phunone.

Another clue we have is the verse in Deuteronomy 2:9 where Moses relates that he was instructed by the Almighty not to incite the Moabites to war.

- The verse implies that the warning was given after they left Phunone, and before they arrived at the wilderness of Moab; evidently, it took place at Ovoth.[7]
- Since they encircled Moab by going along the southern border, and then turning to its eastern border, the natural place for this instruction would have been at the point where they began to encircle Moab at the southwestern corner; evidently, Ovoth was situated there.
- Phunone must have been very close to Moab since from there, the Israelites requested from Moab passageway; evidently, the southwestern corner (and Ovoth) was slightly to the east of Phunone.

—————— Encampment 38 ——————

# IYEI HA'AVARIM (27)

Biblical Reference: Numbers 33:44, 21:11, Deuteronomy 2:13–16

Timeline: 40th year from Exodus, Av, the 5th month

Journey: The Israelites leave Ovoth and travel to Iyei Ha'avarim.

## Event

Moses is told by the Almighty that the Israelites should now[8] pass over Wadi Zared.

## Location

The instruction to pass over Wadi Zared, without first being told to journey there—as we find by Wadi Arnon mentioned later in Deuteronomy 2:24—indicates that Iyei Ha'avarim was located right next to Wadi Zared.

7   It is interesting to note that the words of the verse in Deuteronomy 2:9, "אל תצר את מואב ואל תתגר בם מלחמה—Do not besiege Moab or incite them to war," is an anagram of the words "אלא מאבות אל תצר ותתגר בם מלחמה," which mean "but from Ovoth do not besiege and incite them to war."

8   The word "now" added here, unlike in other places (such as verse 24), is evidently to hint that this instruction was not said at the same time as the instruction in verse 9.

Further information can be gleaned from an apparent contradiction between Numbers and Deuteronomy.

- In Deuteronomy 2:24, Moses is instructed at Iyei Ha'avarim to **pass over** Wadi Zared.
- However, in Numbers 21:12 we are told that following the encampment of Iyei Ha'avarim, the Israelites encamped **in** Wadi Zared.

In reconciliation of the verses, the implication is that both are indeed true. They did pass over Wadi Zared, but further north, the wadi bent around into their line of path, and they encamped there in the wadi itself.

Indeed, when we consult the map, we find about 40 km east of Phunone the Wadi Djoref, which indeed bends around further north. Djoref[9] is actually a continuation of Wadi Hassi, which is commonly identified as Wadi Zared, based on an ancient map found in Madaba, Jordan.[10]

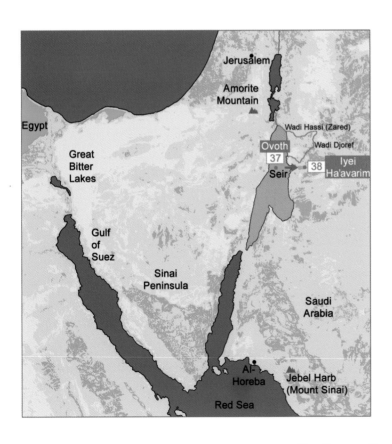

9    It is interesting to note that the numerical value of ג'ורף (Djoref) is the same numerical value as נחל זרד (Wadi Zared), where the apostrophe on the letter ג is taken as the Hebrew letter י.

10   Rabbi Yehudah Landy, *Shalosh Artzos L'Shevi'is* (2014), p. 68.

CHAPTER TWENTY-FOUR

# The Three Decrees

After the Sin of the Spies, exile was decreed on the Israelites. This actually comprised three separate decrees:

- Prohibition of entry into the Holy Land (Numbers 14:30).
- Wandering through the wilderness for 40 years (Numbers 14:29).
- Death in the wilderness during those 40 years (Numbers 14:32) for all the males[1] between the ages of 20 and 60.[2]

Careful study of the verses and guided by Rabbinic Tradition, we are led to the conclusion that the culmination of each decree came at separate times.

## The Prohibition of Entry in the Holy Land

In Numbers 20:22, the verse emphasizes that the whole congregation journeyed from Kadesh and encamped at Hor Hahar.

- *Midrash Tanchuma* explains that this was the congregation that was destined to enter the land of Israel. Why just now?
- Furthermore, this seems to be contradicted by verse 20:1, which also emphasizes the arrival of the whole congregation at the encampment before, at Kadesh. Indeed, *Rashi* there explains that this was to tell us that they were the complete congregation who were destined to live.[3]

1    *Sifri*, Numbers 26:64.

2    *Bava Basra* 121b.

3    In the further encampments, this is not stressed, so if they were already complete at Kadesh, this should not have been stressed again at Hor Hahar.

The answer appears to lie in the careful wording of *Midrash Tanchuma* and is highlighted by *Rashi* in verse 20:1.

- *Midrash Tanchuma* stresses that they were the congregation **destined to enter the land of Israel.**
- Although *Rashi* quotes this in verse 22, in verse 1, he writes differently; that they were the congregation **destined to live.**

Indeed, already at Kadesh, all those who were destined to die from that generation had already died,[4] but the decree of the prohibition to enter Canaan had still not been nullified. This took place evidently after the death of Miriam. The Talmud in *Moed Katan*[5] says that the death of Miriam is mentioned next to the previous chapter about the Red Heifer to teach us that the same way the Red Heifer atones, so too does the death of the righteous. Evidently, the death of Miriam atoned for the decree of not entering the Holy Land, and thus when they came to the next encampment at Hor Hahar, they were now ready to enter the Land of Israel. This is why the verse emphasizes again "the whole congregation."

## The Decree of Death

In Numbers 33, the Torah summarizes the journeys of the Israelites through the 40 years of wandering, focusing just on the encampments but not on events that took place there, with one exception. After mentioning the encampment at Hor Hahar, the Torah quite unexpectedly then spends two complete verses[6] describing the death and burial of Aaron, detailing the exact time it took place and how old Aaron was. The death and burial of Aaron is already described in detail in Numbers 20:23–29, so why is this repeated and why just here? Furthermore, why is the date and age of Aaron at the time of his death brought down here and not earlier in Numbers 20:23–29?

- A vital clue is the description of Aaron here in Numbers 33 as "Aaron the Priest." This seems most strange, as by now there is no ambiguity as to which Aaron is being referred to here, and we surely know that Aaron was the High Priest. Indeed, when

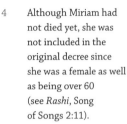

4    Although Miriam had not died yet, she was not included in the original decree since she was a female as well as being over 60 (see *Rashi*, Song of Songs 2:11).

5    28a.

6    38–39.

describing his death in Numbers 20:23–29, the verse refers to him simply as Aaron.

- Apparently, the verse means to point out that the passing of Aaron and the fact that he was a priest had relevance to the wanderings of the Israelites.
- This directs us to the law in Numbers 35:28 that the exile to the city of refuge, which is decreed upon one who kills unintentionally, is nullified with the passing of the High Priest.

The verse in Numbers 33:38 seems to hint that the passing of Aaron the High Priest also brought a culmination to the decree of exile on the whole nation.

The Israelites were destined to remain in exile until the generation of the spies had died. *Midrash Eichah* says that although their deaths were spread out over the 40 years, they only died on one night each year—the 9th of Av, the date of the sin. That year, however, although those remaining from that generation dug their graves, no one died.[7] Evidently, the passing of Aaron the High Priest a few days earlier on the 1st of Av of the 40th year had culminated the decree of death on the generation, effectively heralding an end to the exile.

The fact that the Torah also mentions that Aaron was 123 when he died is possibly to hint that the completion of all those years of righteousness also played a part in the atonement achieved for the Israelites by his passing.

### The Decree of Wandering

Although no one died on the 9th of Av that year and the decree of death had evidently been nullified, the verse in Deuteronomy 2:14 implies that they only ceased to die after they crossed over Nahal Zared, which according to *Taanis* 30b took place on the 15th of Av.

*Midrash Eichah*[8] sheds some light by telling us that after those who dug their graves discovered on the morning of the 9th of Av that they were still alive, they thought that perhaps they had mistaken the date of the New Moon,[9] but they found themselves still alive by the 15th of Av, when they saw

7   *Midrash Eichah*, *Pesichta* 33.
8   Ibid.
9   The first day of the month is determined by the first sighting of the New Moon.

a full moon. They then realized that the decree of death had indeed ended.

But this is still difficult to understand, because a lunar month can only be 29 or 30 days, so they should have realized that the 9th of Av had passed long before the 15th of the month. Furthermore, how does this connect to Nahal Zared?

We can surmise the missing pieces of the puzzle in light of the identification of the site of the graves, the precise path of the Israelites, and the location of Nahal Zared.

We now know the following:

- The graves were situated next to Kadesh Barnea at the southwestern corner of Se'ir.[10]
- From Kadesh Barnea, the Israelites requested from Edom to pass through their land but were refused. Instead, they headed north along the Aravah until they reached Phunone. Then, after Moab also refused, they headed east along the southern border of Moab, and then turned north until Wadi Zared.[11]
- We know from *Taanis* 30b that by the 15th of Av they had already crossed over Wadi Zared. The distance traveled between the two is about 230 km. The average rate of travel is 40 Hebraic miles in one day, and going at this pace would have taken them 6 days to cover that ground (6 × 40 = 240 Hebraic miles = 228 km[12]). Bearing in mind that they did not travel on the Sabbath, they would have likely left Kadesh no later than the 8th of Av.

Evidently, the Israelites left those whom they believed were destined to die at Kadesh and set off to Phunone. On the morning of the 9th, after the ones who remained in Kadesh saw that they had not died, they assumed that there must have been a miscalculation of the New Moon sighting and that the following night was the 9th of Av. However, after surviving the following night too, they realized that they had definitely passed the 9th but could not understand why they had not died. Naturally, they headed off along the path

10  Chapter 22.

11  Chapter 23.

12  One Hebraic mile = 0.95 km (see chapter 1).

of the Israelites in order to reach them and ask Moses what should be done.

By now, the Israelites were at least 80 km ahead of them. In a matter of urgency, traveling can be increased by 25 percent[13] to reach a total of 50 Hebraic miles a day, and this would have allowed them to reach the Israelite camp just as they crossed over Nahal Zared on the 15th.[14] Evidently, after noting their arrival just as full moon had been reached and a new phase of the month had begun without them dying, Moses confirmed there and then that the decree of death must have ended and that they were not going to die. Indeed, that very day, the Almighty spoke to Moses for the first time since the Sin of the Spies, with the same endearment, and the 15th of Av was then declared a day of festivities.[15]

According to *Midrash Eichah*,[16] the same number died each year and thus those who survived the last year amounted to about 16,000 people (600,000/38). According to the Jerusalem Talmud,[17] each year only the ones who turned 60 died, and thus the ones who turned 60 in the 40th year very possibly amounted to tens of thousands. One cannot begin to imagine the exhilaration that the Israelites must have experienced that day, upon seeing so many of their fathers, brothers, family, and friends literally return from their graves!

The verse, however, still needs further qualification as it implies that the **cessation** itself of the deaths took place on this day and not just the **realization of the cessation**. This can be explained as pointed out by Rabbi Pesach Bodenheimer.

Rabbeinu Yonah[18] derives from *Midrash Tehillim* 79 that the atonement of death already begins in the moments before a person dies at the time the fear of death takes hold of him. Evidently the decree of death was not entirely taken away from the remainder of that generation after Aaron died, but instead was fulfilled through the fear of dying. On that day, the fear of death ended and their atonement was completed, and this constituted the complete cessation of the decree of death.

13  *Pesachim* 94a.
14  Barring the Sabbath, this leaves 5 days in which they could cover 250 Hebraic miles (5 × 50 = 250) = 237.5 km.
15  *Taanis* 30b.
16  Ibid.
17  *Bikkurim* 6b.
18  *Shaarei Teshuvah*.

Once the cessation of the decree of death finally took place, the decree of wandering automatically ended, and this came into effect by leaving the wilderness and crossing over Wadi Zared,[19] evidently on the very same day!

## The Song of the Well

With this we can now understand a literal explanation of the verses[20] of the Song of the Well that refer to going from the wilderness to "Matanah" and on to "Nahaliel," and then to "Bamoth" and then to the valley where the mountain overlooks the Yeshimon.

This can now be discerned as referring to the movements of the Israelites from the exile leading up to the events regarding the Well of Miriam.

From the wilderness they went to Nahal Zared, called Matanah, which means "gift"—after the gift of life granted there to the thousands that remained from the generation of the spies.

In chapter 27, we will see the explanation for the continuation of the verse.

## Why Go through Edom?

At Kadesh Barnea on the southwest corner of Se'ir, the Israelites sent a request to Edom,[21] evidently under the instruction from the Almighty,[22] to pass through their land on their journey to Canaan.

Why was this necessary? They could have gone north via the Aravah to the west of Se'ir and, indeed, this is what they did after Edom refused.

This can now be explained. The Israelite camp headed north on the 8th of Av, leaving behind the last of the generation of the spies. Since there was no longer among them anyone from that generation who was destined to die, there was no necessity any more to wander through the wilderness, and they were now fit to pass with dignity through the populated lands.

Edom refused and the Israelites were forced to take the path of the Aravah. However, as Rabbi Pesach Bodenheimer points out, in retrospect, the refusal of the Edomites may have been

19   It is fascinating to note that the letters of the words Nahal Zared (נחל זרד) spell out the words "חל רז נד," which means "the secret of wandering has been effected."

20   Numbers 21:19–20.

21   Numbers 20:14.

22   In Deuteronomy 2:3, Moses relates that he was instructed to head north and to instruct the people to buy food and drink from the Edomites as they pass by. If this meant that they were to head north via the Aravah, they would not have encountered the Edomites at this point because until Phunone, there is no access to the mountainous region of Se'ir. This is also indicated in Numbers 21:4, which says the Israelites headed south from Hor Hahar in order "to encircle the land of Edom." The implication is that they were heading to encircle the southwestern corner of Edom and then pass through Edom from the south.

a blessing in disguise, bringing about the incredible reunion at Nahal Zared. Had the Edomites granted permission, the Moabites may have followed suit, and the Israelites would have headed north through the land of Moab to the straits of Moab. This would have cut them off from the survivors of the generation of spies, who—left with nothing to protect themselves—would surely have been scared to pass through Edom or Moab. They would have been vulnerable to attack and ambush in the long trek around Moab and through Wadi Arnon.

## CHAPTER TWENTY-FIVE

# Divon Gad

---
## Encampment 39
## DIVON GAD (28)
---

Biblical Reference: Numbers 33:45, 21:13, Deuteronomy 2:14–25

Timeline: 40th year from Exodus, 15th of Av, the 5th month

Journey: The Israelites leave Iyei Ha'avarim, pass over Wadi Zared and travel to Divon Gad.

## Event

At the encampment of Divon Gad, the Almighty speaks to Moses for the first time since the decree of exile, with the original level of endearment. That day, the 15th of Av, was then incorporated into the Jewish calendar as a day of festivities.[1]

Moses is told that they would now pass Ar, the country of Moab, and draw close to Ammon but should not incite the Ammonites. They were to journey on that day to Wadi Arnon and cross over it, and the dread of the Israelites would be then instilled into the hearts of the nations.

## Location

In Numbers 21:12, the verse says that the Israelites traveled from Iyei Ha'Avarim and encamped in Wadi Zared. Since we know from Numbers 33:45 that they traveled from

---

1    Taanis 30b.

Iyei Ha'avarim to Divon Gad, it follows that Divon Gad lay in Wadi Zared.

As we saw in chapter 23, Wadi Zared (Djoref) bends around again into the line of the path of the Israelites after they would have crossed the wadi and headed north from Iyei Ha'avarim. Divon Gad was evidently located in the wadi at that point.

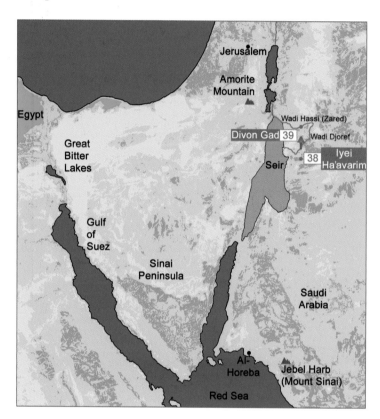

## CHAPTER TWENTY-SIX

# Almon Divlathaimah

---

## Encampment 40
### ALMON DIVLATHAIMAH (29)

Biblical Reference: Numbers 33:46, 21:13, 21–23

Timeline: 40th year from Exodus, after the 15th of Av, the 5th month

Journey: The Israelites leave Divon Gad, travel to Wadi Arnon, and cross over it, and encamp in the wilderness on the edge of Arnon.

## Location

- In Numbers 21:13, the verse says that the Israelites encamped on the other side of Wadi Arnon, because Wadi Arnon lay between Moab and the Amorites.
- Since we know that the Israelites were traveling in a northernly direction, the implication is that they encountered Wadi Arnon to their east, winding down in a south-north direction. In this way, they would have to cross over the wadi, encamping in the wilderness so as not to enter into the territory of Moab.
- The straightforward implication of Judges 11:13 is that Wadi Arnon lies on an east-west plain; evidently, further north the wadi bends round to the west or east.

The Wadi of Arnon is identified by *Kaftor Va'Ferach* as being the present-day Wadi Modjib.[1] Indeed, the wadi goes from east to west and ends in the Dead Sea, but is joined by the present-day Wadi Nuchila coming from the south. This was evidently considered part of the Biblical Wadi of Arnon and served as the eastern border of Moab and the western border of the Amorites.

Looking for a likely perimeter of Moab due north of the Israelite path, we find a wadi joining Wadi Nuchila as it crosses the west-east road from Carak to Katrana. This is a likely point for the Israelites to have turned north-east and crossed Wadi Arnon here.

The verse in Deuteronomy 2:18 indicates that before they encamped, they passed along the border of Ar,[2] and Numbers 21:28 indicates that at least one part of Ar incorporated the highest point of the wadi. Indeed, if the Israelites encamped just after they passed over the wadi at this point, the head of the encampment, which was 12 Hebraic miles long[3]

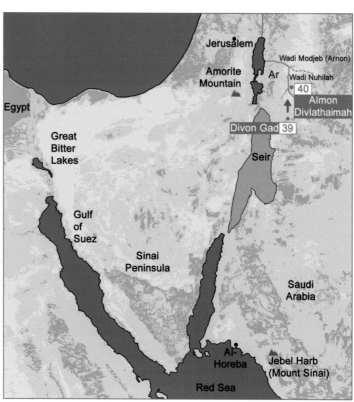

1    Chap. 47, p. 131.
2    See also Deuteronomy 2:29. Both verses indicate that Ar was not the name of a city but the name of the country.
3    *Eruvin* 55b, based on Numbers 33:49.

(11.4 km), would be about 10 km away from the highest point in the wadi.

## Event

Moses sends messengers to Sichon, the king of the Amorites, asking for permission to pass through their land, but Sichon refuses and gathers all his people in preparation for battle against the Israelites.

## CHAPTER TWENTY-SEVEN

# The Miracle at Nahal Arnon

In Numbers 21, after relating the encampment after crossing Wadi Arnon, the text digresses with several obscure verses, followed by describing the "Song of the Well" that was sung at the time.

*Midrash Tanchuma* explains that the verses and song are referring to a miracle that happened shortly before they crossed the wadi and was revealed to them at the encampment following the crossing.

The Amorites, taking note of the path of the Israelites, believed that the Israelites would head through Wadi Arnon between Moab and the Amorites, and they consequently lay in ambush in caves on the western side of the wadi. However, as the Israelites approached, the land of the Amorites shifted toward them as if coming out to greet them. The effect of the shift was that the eastern side of the wadi pressed against the western side. On the eastern side there were protrusions in the mountain and as the two sides embraced, the protrusions slotted into the caves on the western side and crushed the Amorites.

The Israelites came along afterward and actually came out of the wadi on the Amorite side, unaware of what happened. However, the Well of Miriam washed out the caves and the dismembered limbs became visible, and the Israelites then realized the salvation that had taken place and sung the "Song of the Well."

Following the literal explanation of the Song of the Well, mentioned in a previous chapter, the continuation of the verse that refers to the Israelites going to Nahaliel and then to Bamoth and then to the valley next to the mountain that overlooks the Yeshimon is referring to the movements of the Israelites with regard to the Well of Miriam.

After leaving Matanah, they went to Nahal Arnon, which is called here Nahaliel, meaning "the wadis (or rivers) of the Almighty"—after the miracle that took place in the wadi together with the revelation caused by the Well of Miriam.

From there they went to Bamoth, which means "the heights," referring to the cliffs of Arnon, where they saw testimony of the salvation.

From there, they traveled to Harei Ha'avarim, to the valley next to Pe'or and overlooking Yeshimon. The reference to looking over Yeshimon hints to the verse in Numbers 23:28, when Balaam comes to the top of Pe'or to look over the Yeshimon at the camp of the Israelites in order to curse them. From there he praised the tents of the Israelites that were set up between the flowing streams (Numbers 24:5–6), evidently referring to the separate channels that flowed down from the Well of Miriam to each of the tribes, as well as surrounding the whole encampment and watering the whole Yeshimon.[1]

## Location

Can we locate the site of this great miracle at Nahal Arnon? We have two further clues.

- The verse in Numbers 21:15 indicates that the site was situated by Ar, and verse 28 indicates that Ar comprised the highest point of the wadi.
- *Midrash Tanchuma* says that one person could speak to another from either side of the wadi, and the distance (evidently walking distance[2]) between the two sides of the two peaks was 7 Hebraic miles.[3]

When we take a look at the map, it is quite easy to identify the highest point in the wadi, which is just southeast of the Mujib Dam.

Indeed, on the western side there are caves, and on the western side one can discern that set into the rock face are

1    *Tosefta, Sukkah* 3:3.
2    If the distance was 7 Hebraic miles as the crow flies, it would be quite impossible to speak to one another.
3    See chapter 1, where 7 Hebraic Miles = 7 × 0.95 km = 6.65 km.

indeed giant protrusions. The shape of the western cliffs almost mirrors the shape of the eastern cliff, and they could fit together almost like a glove if the eastern flank would shift southward toward the western flank. The Israelites were slated to pass in between, in the wadi, as described by *Rashi*.

Finally, the walking distance between the two is indeed 7 Hebraic miles!

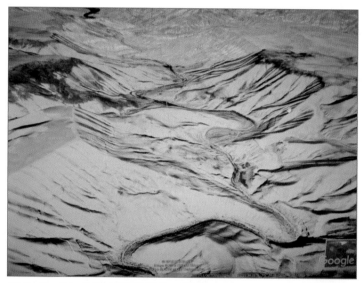

Attribution: Google Earth CNES/Airbus, 2019

Attribution: Google Earth CNES/Airbus, 2019

Attribution: Google Earth CNES/Airbus, 2019

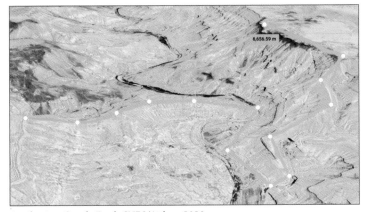
Attribution: Google Earth CNES/Airbus, 2020

## CHAPTER TWENTY-EIGHT

# Conquest of Trans-Jordan

Biblical Reference: Numbers 21:21–35, 32,
Deuteronomy 2:26–3:22

Timeline: 40th year from Exodus, between Av and Shevat,
the 5th and 11th months

## Conquest of Sichon

Sichon gathers his army and heads for the wilderness, where the Israelites are encamped. The two sides meet at Yahtzah, and Sichon and his army and people are totally destroyed. The Israelites take possession of the Amorite land from Wadi Arnon going north to Wadi Yabok, and from the Jordan River going east to the wilderness, but do not enter into the land of Amon. Among the cities captured are those that have maintained their name until this day, such as Heshbon, Aroer, Maidebah, and Divon.

## The Wadi Yabok

- The Wadi Yabok is also mentioned in Genesis 32:23, when Jacob returns from Haran with his family and crosses over the Yabok just before his encounter with Esau.
- Following that encounter, Jacob travels to Succoth, and then on to Shechem. Evidently, Succoth was near Wadi Yabok, and north or parallel with Shechem.
- The Jerusalem Talmud[1] lists Succoth as part of the realm of Sichon and identifies it as Tirelah. This seems

1    *Shevi'is* 25b.

synonymous with Dir Allah,[2] just north of the Wadi El Zarka, and parallel with Shechem, at the point it crosses the straits of the Jordan River.

- Indeed, *Kaftor Va'Ferach*[3] identifies Yabok as the Wadi El Zarka.

## The Land of Amon

- In Numbers 21:24, we are told that the Israelites took over the land from Wadi Arnon until Wadi Yabok, which was the border of Amon.
- However, in a seemingly conflicting verse in Deuteronomy 2:37, we are told that they left the immediate area next to Yabok, as that was also part of Amon territory.

In light of the identification of the Wadi Yabok, we can now reconcile the two.

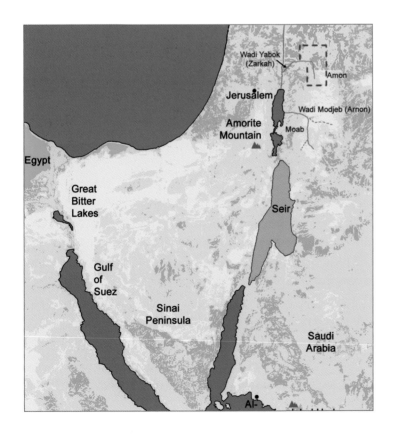

2    Pointed out by Rabbi Yehudah Landy, *Shalosh Artzos L'Shevi'is* (2014), p. 197.

3    Chap. 47.

The Wadi El Zarka runs from east to west, ending in the Jordan River. However, it is joined by a tributary running from south to north, about 25 km east from the Jordan River.

Evidently, the verse in Numbers is referring to the west-east section of the Yabok, which acted as the border of Amon, but the south-north tributary, which also comprised the Biblical Yabok, was actually within the border of Amon as the Amonites maintained the neighboring territory to the west. This is what the verse in Deuteronomy is referring to. The verse in Deuteronomy also refers to the cities in the mountains, and indeed this part is a mountainous area.

## The Flame of Kiryath Sichon

In Numbers 21:28, the verse refers to a flame sparking out from the city of Sichon that devoured the territory of Ar at the heights of Arnon. Now, taking a look at the map, we can understand the verse to be speaking metaphorically about the strip of land coming out of the Amorite bloc, shaped like a flame, between Yabok and Arnon, beginning at the heights of Arnon, and going south alongside the wadi, which was taken over by Sichon.

## The Conquest of Bashan

After taking over the Amorite territory, the Israelites advanced northward toward Bashan and encountered Og and his army at Edre'i and destroyed them, inheriting the territory from Wadi Arnon until Mount Hermon, which comprised the Gilad and the Bashan. Edre'i is identified with Derah in present-day Syria.[4]

The land of the Amorites and half the Gilad was given to the tribes of Reuben and Gad, and the other half of Gilad and the Bashan was given to half the tribe of Menasheh.

4    Rabbi Yehudah Landy,
*Shalosh Artzos L'Shevi'is*
(2014), p. 179.

## CHAPTER TWENTY-NINE

# Harei Ha'avarim

---
### Encampment 41
## HAREI HA'AVARIM (30)

Biblical Reference: Numbers 33:47, 27:1–11, 15–23, Deuteronomy 3:23–29

Timeline: 40th year from Exodus, after conquest of Trans-Jordan

Journey: The Israelites leave Almon Divlathaimah and travel to Harei Ha'avarim.

## Event

The daughters of Zelophehad, who died in the wilderness, come to Moses and Elazar and request a portion in the Land of Israel instead of their father. Moses consults the Almighty and is told that, indeed, they rightfully deserve two portions in the land: that of their father and part of the portion of their grandfather who also came out of Egypt.

Moses, after being told to grant inheritance to the daughters of Zelophehad, entertains the idea that perhaps his sin has been forgiven and he will be permitted to enter the land of Canaan and divide it up among the Israelites after the conquest,[1] but the Almighty informs him that the former decree still stands. Moses then entreats the Almighty that He appoint a new leader who will be able to cater to the

---

1   *Bamidbar Rabbah* 21:14.

requirements of the Israelites, and is told that he should prepare Joshua. After first ensuring the needs of the Israelites,[2] Moses then entreats the Almighty that he himself be granted permission to cross over the Jordan River, and that he may see the "good land." His request of entering the land is refused, but he is told that he may see the land by ascending to the top of the mountain, which he does then and there.[3]

## Location

The verse in Deuteronomy 33:47 says that the Israelites encamped at Harei Ha'avarim, which means "the Mountains of Passing Over." It also says that in front of them stood Nebo. The verse in Deuteronomy 3:29 says they stayed in the wadi, opposite Pe'or.

Looking at the map we can discern the place of encampment.

- Mount Nebo, still called this today, is one of a series of mountains joined together by wadis between them.

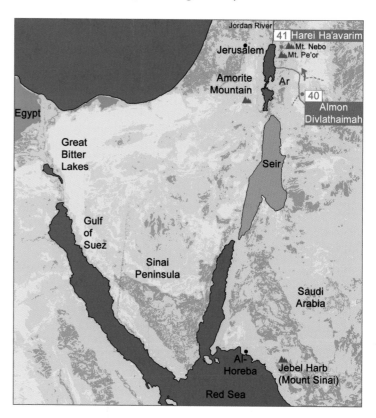

2    *Sifri* 138.
3    *Malbim*, Numbers
      27:12.

- It is these wadis that offer a passageway into Canaan via the Jordan River, and that is evidently the reason behind their name.
- "In front," according to the Torah, is to the east[4]; indeed the wadi next to Mount Nebo bends round to the west of the mountain, so if they encamped along this wadi, in front of them would indeed lie Nebo.
- Evidently, on the adjacent mountain to Nebo lay the idol Baal Pe'or.

This identification now resolves the *Midrash Tanchuma*[5] that states that just three mountains were not flattened by the Clouds of Glory—Mount Sinai, Hor Hahar, and Mount Nebo. It does not include the Mountains of Ha'avarim, which were also not flattened, as indicated in Numbers 33:47. This can now be understood because the Mountains of Ha'avarim were none other than Mount Nebo itself and its extension on the other side of the wadi.

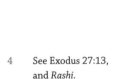

4   See Exodus 27:13, and *Rashi*.
5   Numbers, *Chukas* 14.

## CHAPTER THIRTY

# When Did the Episode of Baal Pe'or Take Place?

In Numbers 22–24, the Torah relates how Balak hires Balaam to curse the Israelites. Balaam tries three times, but instead of curses, blessings emanate from his mouth. Balak sends Balaam away in disgust, but before going, Balaam prophesies what will happen in the End of Days. The next chapter relates how the Israelites were seduced by the Moabites into serving Baal Pe'or, the consequential death of twenty-four thousand Israelites, and the act of zealousness of Phinehas that brought an end to the plague. Numbers 31:16 states that the seduction came as a result of Balaam's advice, and is hinted at in Balaam's final conversation with Balak in Numbers 24:14.[1]

- One of the places Balaam was taken to in order to curse the Israelites was Pe'or, which overlooked the Yeshimon.
- At the time of the episode of Baal Pe'or, the Israelites were dwelling in Shittim.
- The straightforward implication is that it must have taken place at the last encampment by the straits of Moab, since there the encampment stretched from Beth Hayeshimoth until Shittim, as indicated in Numbers 33:49 and Joshua 3:1.

However, according to one view in *Bechoros* 5b, the "Shittim" referenced with regard to Baal Pe'or was not the name of the place but a description of the levity that brought

1   *Sanhedrin* 106a.

about the seduction. This allows for the possibility that the episode of Baal Pe'or took place in the encampment before, at Harei Ha'avarim, which we saw in the previous chapter was located in the valley next to Pe'or and Mount Nebo.

This in turn allows for a straightforward understanding of the verses describing the final rebukes of Moses to the Israelites.

- At the beginning of Deuteronomy 1:3, Moses begins a lengthy rebuke on the 1st of the 11th month in the 40th year, which stretches to the end of Chapter 4.
- It opens by saying that it took place in the land of Moab and closes by saying that the laws mentioned were said in the valley opposite Pe'or.
- Included in Chapter 4 is reference to the episode of Baal Pe'or.

We can now say that this rebuke actually took place in the valley opposite Pe'or, at Harei Ha'avarim. The calling together of the Israelites at the beginning of Chapter 5 then marks the start of another rebuke at a later date, at the final encampment in the straits of Moab.

## CHAPTER THIRTY-ONE

# Arvoth Moab

---

Encampment 42

## ARVOTH MOAB (42)

**Biblical Reference:** Numbers 33:48–49, the book of Deuteronomy

**Timeline:** 40th year from Exodus, after conquest of Trans-Jordan

**Journey:** The Israelites leave Harei Ha'avarim, and journey to Arvoth Moab, and encamp between Beth Hayeshimoth and Avel Hashittim.

### Event

Moses explains the laws of the Torah to the Israelites and warns them of what will befall them if they turn astray. His final day arrives, the 7th day of the 12th month of Adar, and under the instruction of the Almighty, Moses gives over the authority of leadership to Joshua. Moses ascends the summit of Mount Nebo, and looks across the Jordan at the Holy Land,[1] and then dies on the mountain.[2] He is buried in the wadi, opposite Pe'or.[3]

The wadi referred to was evidently the wadi between Mount Nebo and the adjacent mountain south of Nebo, and thus opposite Pe'or, as we saw in the last chapter.

[1] The verse says that he saw until *"yam ha'acharon,"* which literally means until "the latter sea," but can also be translated as until "the last day." Indeed, *Sifri* informs us that Moses saw all the events that would happen to the Children of Israel until the day of Resurrection. It is interesting to note that Moses was instructed to ascend the mountain but not specifically to go to the summit, and this evidently Moses did of his own accord to maximize his view of the Holy Land. It is perhaps in the merit of this final act of diligence that Moses was granted not only to see the land once again but the whole future of the nation.

[2] Deuteronomy 32:50.

[3] Ibid., 34:6.

## Location

- The *Beraisa*[4] tells us that the encampment of the Israelites was 12 Hebraic miles by 12 Hebraic miles.
- We know from Numbers 23:28 that Pe'or looked over the Yeshimon, and Pe'or, we have already learned, was on the adjacent mountain south of Mount Nebo.
- We also know from Joshua[5] that the spies were sent to Jericho from Shittim, and also that the crossing of the Jordan took place from Shittim, so evidently Shittim was opposite Jericho on the other side of the Jordan.
- Indeed, there are precisely 12 Hebraic miles (11.4) km[6] going north from the northern edge of the Dead Sea and next to Pe'or until parallel with the established site of ancient Jericho called Tel-Jericho.[7]

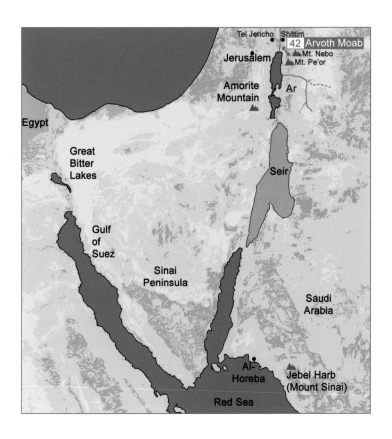

4    Brought down in the Talmud, *Sotah* 13b.

5    2:1, 3:1.

6    See chapter 1, note 10, that 1 Hebraic mile = 0.95 km.

7    *Rashi* says that Avel Hashittim was the plain beside Shittim, so evidently the encampment ended just at the end of Shittim next to the plain of Shittim.

# Mapping Out the Hebrew Letters for the Word "Exile"

After tracing the path of the Israelites throughout their sojourn in the 40 years of exile, I took note of a most remarkable phenomena.

As we have seen, the period of wanderings comprised four distinct phases. Looking at the pattern of encampments of the first phase, which comprised five consecutive encampments, the locations, when joined together, seemed to resemble the form of the Hebrew letter ג. The next phase, also consisting of five[1] consecutive encampments, take the form of the letter ל. The next five take the form of the letter ו, and the last five,[2] culminating in the encampment by Nahal Zared,[3] the form of the letter ת. The four letters together spell out in the right order the Hebrew word for exile, גלות, as can be seen below.

The chance of five consecutive encampments forming anything remotely like a Hebrew letter is surely unlikely to say the least. The discovery that another five consecutive encampments after that resemble another letter and another five after that a different letter, and a further five yet another letter, and altogether produce a word in that order that has relevance to the whole period of wandering is quite astonishing.[4]

---

1  Following the encampments of Haradah and Makheiloth, which were evidently not originally planned but were necessitated by the episode of Korah.

2  Apart from the encampment of Hor Hahar, which was evidently not originally planned as part of the exile but were necessitated by the Sin of Mei Merivah.

3  Iyei Ha'avarim, the last encampment of the exile as we saw in chapter 23.

4  It is also fascinating to note that the encampment of Etzion Gaver completes the letter ו. In chapter 12, we discovered that Etzion Gaver was the site of the sin of the *mekoshesh*. Indeed, the *Zohar* (at the beginning of *Parashas Shelach*) says that his sin was related to the Kabbalistic symbol of the letter ו, and hinted at in the words of the Torah "בחטאו מת" (Numbers 27:3), i.e., "בחטא ו מת" (that he died because of the sin of the letter *vav*).

*(continued on next page)*

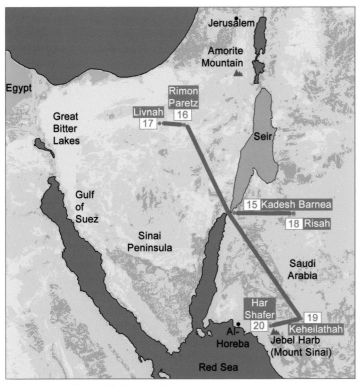

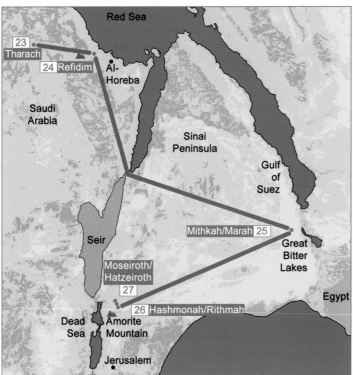

*(continued from previous page)*

Furthermore, the letter ת ends at Iyei Ha'avarim. In chapter 24, we saw that the verse in Numbers 21:18, "מן המדבר מתנה—from the wilderness to Matanah," is referring to the journey from Iyei Ha'avarim at the end of the exile, and the letters can be read "מן המדבר מן ה'ת," which means "from the wilderness they journeyed to the place after the 'ת." It is further fascinating to note that the letter ת begins to be mapped out at Kadesh, the encampment where Miriam was buried and is perhaps hinted at in the words about Miriam in Exodus 15:20, which say, "את התף בידה," which can mean, "the letter *taf* is next to her."

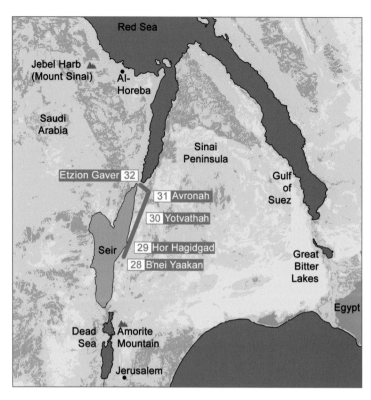

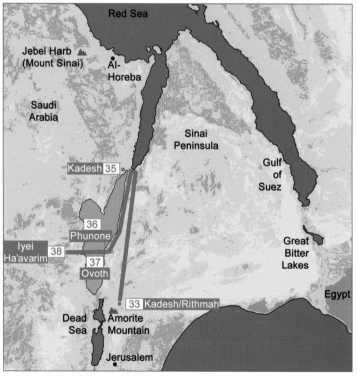

# The Ark of the Covenant and the Ark of the Testimony

As mentioned in chapter 20, the Jerusalem Talmud tells us that there were two Arks.[1] One Ark was made by Moses and the other one by Betzalel. The Ark of Moses was made of wood and initially housed the Second Tablets of stone, but following the setting up of the Tabernacle they were transferred to the Ark of Betzalel, also made of wood but with an outer and inner box made of gold, together with a golden top and two Cherubim. The Ark of Moses housed the broken Tablets of stone, and it was this Ark that went a path of three days before the Israelites to map out their route. The Ark of Betzalel resided in the Tabernacle.

We can now discern that there were two different names given to each Ark, and this reveals a startling insight as to what exactly happened when the first Tablets were smashed.

- The Ark of the Tabernacle is consistently referred to as the Ark of the **Testimony**,[2] however the Ark of Moses is referred to as the Ark of the **Covenant of the Almighty**.[3]
- They were evidently so called after the Tablets of stone that they housed.
- We find that the first Tablets were called the Tablets of the **Testimony**[4] and the Tablets of the **Covenant**,[5] but the second set were only called the Tablets of the **Testimony**.[6]

1   *Sotah* 35a.
2   Exodus 25:22, 26:34, 30:26, 39:35, 40:3,5,21; Numbers 4:5, 7:89.
3   Numbers 10:33, 14:44.
4   Exodus 31:18, 32:15.
5   Deuteronomy 9:9,11,15.
6   Exodus 34:29.

- In the smashing of the first Tablets, the miraculous handwritten letters of the Almighty flew heavenward,[7] and the testimony the Tablets carried was understandably lost. However, it now becomes apparent that the Covenant made with them[8] was never broken, and they therefore maintained their status of the Tablets of the **Covenant**. Consequently, the Ark that housed them was called the Ark of the **Covenant of the Almighty**.[9]

- The second set of stones were imbued once again with the handwritten letters of the Almighty,[10] and thus they now became the Tablets of the **Testimony**, and the Ark that housed them, the Ark of the **Testimony**.

- The second Tablets and, in turn, the Ark that housed them, were not called the Tablets of the Covenant and the Ark of the Covenant, because no Covenant was made with them, since the original Covenant made with the first Tablets was never broken.

This sheds further light on many intriguing verses and allows us to trace the path of each Ark throughout Biblical history, allowing for further insight into the purposes of each one of them.

### Who Carried the Ark and When?

In Deuteronomy 10:8, the verse describes the designation of the Levites to carry the Ark, as well as service in the Tabernacle. The verse begins with, "At that time," and the simple indication is that it refers to the same year in which they were in Yotvathah, mentioned in the previous verse. In chapter 19, we saw this was 20 years after the Sin of the Golden Calf, at the time when the Levites were cleansed and atoned to be substitutes of the firstborn in the service of the Tabernacle.

But this is problematic: The verse mentions the task of carrying of the Ark, however, we know from Numbers 10:21[11] that the Levites already began to carry it just after the Sin of the Golden Calf in the 2nd year from the Exodus.

7   *Targum Yonasan*, Exodus 32:19.
8   Deuteronomy 4:13, 5:2–4, 9:9.
9   See *Sifri*, Numbers 10:33.
10  Exodus 34:1, Deuteronomy 10:4.
11  The verse actually says that the Levite family of Kehath carried "the *mikdash*," but *Eruvin* 2b qualifies it to mean the Ark.

However, this can now be understood, as the verse in Deuteronomy specifies, "the Ark of the **Covenant of the Almighty**." Indeed, the Ark of the Tabernacle—the Ark of the **Testimony**—was carried by the Levites already from the 2nd year, but the carrying of the Ark of Moses by the Levites—the Ark of the **Covenant of the Almighty**, which housed the broken Tablets—was only instigated after the Levites had been cleansed and atoned 20 years later.

The verse in Numbers 10:21 states that the duty of carrying the Ark of the Testimony was given over to the family of Kehath, but the verse in Deuteronomy 10:8 does not specify which of the Levites would carry the Ark of the **Covenant of the Almighty**. However, we know that the second part of the verse is referring to the Kohanim,[12] which suggests that the first part is too.

- Indeed, we find in Deuteronomy 31:9 that Moses gives over a Sefer Torah to the **Kohanim**, the sons of Levi, the carriers of the Ark of the Covenant of the Almighty.
- We also find that at the crossing of the Jordan,[13] the **Kohanim** were instructed to carry the Ark of the **Covenant of the Almighty**, and by the conquest of Jericho, Joshua also instructed the **Kohanim** to carry the Ark of the **Covenant**.[14]
- Furthermore, at the consecration of the Temple, the **Kohanim** carried the Ark of the **Covenant of the Almighty**.[15]

## By Which Ark Was the Sefer Torah Placed?

Just before Moses dies, Moses writes a Sefer Torah and instructs the Levites to put it beside the Ark in order to serve as testimony to future generations. The Ark here is referred to as the Ark of the **Covenant of the Almighty**. This implies that it was placed by the Ark of Moses next to the broken Tablets and not by the Ark of the Tabernacle with the second Tablets of stone.

12   *Arachin* 11a.
13   Joshua 3:6.
14   Ibid., 6:6.
15   Kings I 8:3.

## Which Ark Split the Waters of the Jordan?

In Joshua 3 and 4, the verse relates in detail how the waters of the Jordan split before the Ark.

- Throughout, the verse refers to the Ark as the Ark of the **Covenant of the Almighty**,
- However, verse 4:16 refers to the same Ark as the Ark of the **Testimony**.

This can now be understood as, evidently, the Ark of Moses—which housed the broken Tablets—was indeed involved in the split, but this Ark is also referred to here as the Ark of the **Testimony**, since Moses placed his Sefer Torah there to serve as testimony for the future generations.

## The Ark That Encircled Jericho

When the Israelites came to Jericho just after they crossed the Jordan, they found Jericho locked in by a towering wall encompassing the city. The Almighty instructed Joshua that the Israelite army should encircle the city with the Ark for seven days and then, on the seventh day, encircle seven times followed by the blowing of shofars in front of the Ark. After doing so, the wall miraculously sank suddenly into the ground, and the Israelites captured the city.

Once again, the Ark is referred to as the Ark of the **Covenant of the Almighty**, indicating that it was the Ark of Moses with the broken Tablets that was used.

## The Ark Captured by the Philistines

In the days of Samuel, the Israelites went out to war against the Philistines with the Ark, but it was captured by the Philistines. The verse refers to the Ark as the Ark of the **Covenant of the Almighty**,[16] indicating that it was the Ark of Moses that housed the broken Tablets.[17] However, after the Ark was captured, the verse no longer refers to it by this name, only by the name "Ark of the Almighty."[18] This can be explained, as *Midrash Yalkut Shimoni*[19] says that Saul grabbed the Tablets from Goliath and fled. Since the Tablets of the Covenant were no longer inside, the verse no longer refers to it as the Ark of the **Covenant of the Almighty**.

16 Samuel I 4:3,5.
17 Indeed, this is implied in *Sifrei*, Deuteronomy 11:10.
18 For example, 4:11,13,17,18,19,21,22.
19 Samuel I 4:12.

## The Return of the Tablets to the Ark

The Ark remained by the Philistines, but wherever they took it to, the inhabitants were smitten with death and disease. Eventually, after seven months, they sent the Ark back on an unmanned wagon to Beth Shemesh with compensation. The people of Beth Shemesh were happy at seeing the Ark directed to them by itself in this supernatural way, but seeing the Ark in the state of being unduly unaccompanied proved to their detriment[20] and many died. Out of fear of further retribution, they asked the people of Kiryath Yearim to take it from them. They did so and the Ark remained in Kiryath Yearim for 20 years.[21] King David then attempted to bring back the Ark to the City of David. However, on the way, Oozah, who was leading the wagon, stretched out and took hold of the Ark at one point when it moved suddenly, out of fear of it falling, and he died on the spot.

It is explained in *Sotah*[22] that Oozah should have known from Joshua 4:11 that the Ark carried its carriers, as demonstrated in the crossing of the Jordan, and certainly did not need the help of Oozah to carry it. On seeing what happened, David refrained from taking the Ark to the City of David and left it at the house of Oved the Edomite for three months. In those three months, Oved the Edomite saw blessing come to himself and all his household, and on hearing this, David brought the Ark to the City of David with celebrations.[23]

Throughout, the verse refers to the Ark as the Ark of the **Almighty**, however in Chronicles I,[24] when it was taken from the house of Oved the Edomite, it is referred to once again as the Ark of the **Covenant of the Almighty**. Evidently, David returned the Tablets to the Ark at the house of Oved the Edomite,[25] and this resulted in the forthcoming blessing to him and his household.[26]

## The Ark in the Temple

At the consecration of the first Temple, the verse describes the Kohanim bringing the Ark into the Holy of Holies. One would expect that this was surely the Ark of the Testimony,

20  See Samuel I 6:19. *Tanna D'bei Eliyahu*, chap. 11, says they should have covered themselves with their shawls and come toward the Ark and bowed before it.

21  Samuel I 6–7:2.

22  35a.

23  Samuel II 6.

24  15:25,26,28,29.

25  Although at the time of the crossing of the Jordan, the Tablets were in the Ark, while at the time Oozah took hold of the Ark they were evidently not, Oozah should still have realized that even without having the Tablets, the Ark could carry itself, as hinted in the verse in Joshua. There it is referred to just as the Ark of **the Almighty** when describing that it carried its carriers—and not the Ark of the **Covenant of the Almighty**.

26  Rabbi Pesach Bodenheimer offers an explanation why just at this time the Tablets were transferred to the Ark. Evidently, after they were saved by Saul, the Tablets were kept close to the Tabernacle (as we find that the Ark was in Shiloh before it was captured, Samuel I 1:3). When the Ark was later returned to Beth Shemesh and Kiryath Yearim, they were not returned to the Ark since it was not fitting to move them to a temporary abode.

*(continued on next page)*

which housed the second set of Tablets, and had stood in the Holy of Holies in the Tabernacle.

- However, intriguingly, the verse begins by describing the great assembly of Solomon that accompanied the carrying of the Ark of the **Covenant of the Almighty** from the **City of David** to the Temple, which we saw refers to the Ark of Moses.
- The verse continues to describe that the **Kohanim** brought into the Holy of Holies the Ark of the **Covenant of the Almighty**.
- It further states that in this Ark lay the Tablets of the **Covenant**.

The straightforward implication is that it was in fact the Ark of Moses that was placed in the Holy of Holies in the Temple, and the Golden Ark of Betzalel was evidently hidden along with the Tabernacle,[27] and possibly, all the other vessels.[28] This would also explain why Solomon made two new Cherubim,[29] as the Ark of Moses did not have any Cherubim.

*(continued from previous page)*

King David wanted to unite the Ark with the Tablets of the Covenant but intended to do so at the place fitting for the Ark, in the City of David. At the time the Ark was taken from Kiryath Yearim, the Tablets were evidently taken from where they had been kept to be reunited with the Ark. When the tragedy of Oozah took place, David feared taking the Ark to the City of David, but nonetheless left the Tablets in the Ark by Oved, so that they would not have been moved in vain. The blessing that was forthcoming demonstrated that this was indeed the right decision.

27 *Tosefta Sotah* 13:1, which implies that the Ark was not hidden, is evidently following the differing opinion brought down in the Jerusalem Talmud, *Sotah* 35a, that there was only one Ark, which had two names, the Ark of the **Testimony** and the Ark of the **Covenant of the Almighty**. This is also the indication of the *Beraisa* brought in the Babylonian Talmud, *Bava Basra* 14a.

28 According to one opinion in the *Beraisa* in *Menachos* 99a, the Table and Menorah of the Tabernacle were also used in the Temple.

29 Kings I 6:23–28.

# APPENDIX C

# The Southern Border of Canaan

I n chapter 23, we discovered that the encampment of Phunone is identifiable with Phainon, just north of the Wadi Faidan, which cuts across the mountain of Se'ir about 60 km south of the Dead Sea. Since we know that the Israelites were not granted access through Edom, this would imply that the territory of Edom did not go further north of the Wadi Faidan.

This presents a problem:

- The verse in Numbers 34:3 says that the southern border of Canaan given to the Israelites was from the southwest corner of the Dead Sea.
- The same verse also says that it began from the wilderness of Tzin, next to Edom, implying that Edom stretched further north than the Wadi Phaidan up until the corner of the Dead Sea.

However, this can be resolved by saying that the verse, in mentioning the wilderness of Tzin that is on the corner of Edom, just means to identify the wilderness of Tzin but not where the border of Canaan started. The verse, in describing the southern border of Canaan, beginning from the wilderness of Tzin, is actually referring to the northeastern corner of the wilderness—not next to Edom. The reference of Edom next to the wilderness of Tzin is referring to the southeastern corner of the wilderness, and is there just to identify which wilderness the verse is talking about, rather than the starting point of the southern border.

Furthermore, we can actually deduce another meaning to the verse, whereby, in mentioning the wilderness of Tzin, it is not referring to the beginning of the southern border at all but the southern corner.

- The verse itself seems problematic, as the whole phrase about the wilderness of Tzin and Edom seems redundant, since the verse anyway stipulates that the southern border begins from the southwestern corner of the Dead Sea.
- The term used for southern border in this phrase is *"pe'as negev."*
- Although *pe'as negev* can mean "side" or "border"[1] of the south, it can also mean "corner"[2] of the south.
- Evidently, before entering into the details of the precise boundary of the southern border from the

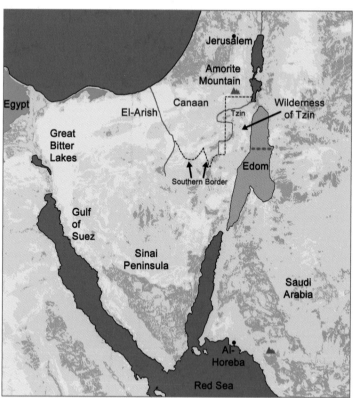

Southern Border of Canaan

1    As we find, for example, in Exodus 27:9.
2    As we find, for example, in Leviticus 19:27.

Dead Sea, the verse opens with a general outline that, unlike the other borders, which were more or less straight, the southern border was different, with one corner bulging to the south.

- The verse identifies this protruding corner as being in the southwestern corner of the southern border, starting from the end of the wilderness of Tzin, whose eastern side was next to Edom.

The Wadi Tzin is still called so today, and the wilderness of Tzin indeed stretches from the wadi in the west until Se'ir in the east and south of Wadi Phaidan.

This would basically mean that anywhere east of the Wadi of Tzin is not part of the land of Canaan given to the Israelites. This has important halachic ramifications, especially with regard to produce of the up-and-coming *shemittah* year, beginning in the autumn of the year 2021.[3]

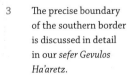

3 The precise boundary of the southern border is discussed in detail in our *sefer Gevulos Ha'aretz*.

# The Name "Kadesh Barnea"

We saw in chapter 2 that there were actually two distinct places called Kadesh Barnea. One was at the southwestern corner of the Dead Sea, and this was the place where the spies were sent out from. Another Kadesh Barnea was on the southwestern corner of Mount Se'ir, just east of the top of the Gulf of Aqaba close to Eilath, and this was the place where the Israelites resided for 19 years following the Sin of the Spies. In chapter 21, we discovered that this was the place where the generation of the spies was buried, and the place where Moses sent messengers to request passageway from Edom.

Both places were sometimes referred to as Kadesh, and sometimes referred to as Kadesh Barnea. We can now discern that both places were not their original names but were called so by the Torah.

The Kadesh Barnea at the corner of the Dead Sea was also called by the Torah Rithmah.[1] This was evidently its original name, as we saw that it is called by the name Rothem until today.

When Moses sent the messengers to Edom, he told them to tell Edom that the Israelites were residing in "Kadesh, a city by the corner of your border." The fact that he emphasized the words "a city" and didn't say simply that they were in "Kadesh, on the corner of your border," implies that the Edomites did not readily recognize a Kadesh on the corner of their border, rather a city with a different name.

1    Numbers 33:18.

If Kadesh Barnea was not the original name of either of these two places, this raises several questions:

- Why does the Torah refer to these places by this name?
- Why does the Torah refer to both by the same name?
- Why is it sometimes referred to as Kadesh and sometimes Kadesh Barnea?
- Why was it so important for Moses, in sending a request to Edom, to refer to the city by the name Kadesh and not by its original name?

The verse in Numbers 20:13 sheds much light on the matter.

The verse says that the Almighty was sanctified (ויקדש) by Mei Merivah. *Rashi* explains that this is in accordance with the verse in Leviticus 10:3, which says that the Almighty will be sanctified through his close ones. The meting out of punishment to those close to the Almighty brings awe and sanctification of the Almighty upon everyone else.

In chapter 13, we discovered that the Sin of Mei Merivah took place at the Kadesh Barnea by the corner of the Dead Sea. *Rashi* says that the name Kadesh was evidently given to the place because of the sanctification of the Almighty that was destined to take place there.[2]

Going one step further, it would seem that the other name Kadesh, given to the place on the southwestern corner of Edom, was for the same reason. This was where the punishment was meted out to the six hundred thousand Israelites of the generation of the spies. These were the people who witnessed the greatest revelation of the Almighty ever, described by the verse[3] as an audience "face-to-face with the Almighty." The Torah considers these people as close to the Almighty, and they accordingly brought awe and sanctity to the Almighty at this place. Accordingly, the name Kadesh given to the place on the corner of the Dead Sea was not just because of the sanctity brought about through Moses and Aaron, but also because of the sanctity brought about by the decree of punishment declared on the generation of the spies at this place.

2    Genesis 14:17.
3    Deuteronomy 5:4.

Moses may have specifically referred to the name Kadesh in his request to the Edomites in order to hint to them that the sanctity of the place was now complete; all those destined to die had already died there, and the Israelites were now ready to enter into the Holy Land.

In our study, *Gevulos Ha'aretz*, we discovered that there is actually another Kadesh Barnea, close to the Wadi El Arish, and this is referenced in Numbers 34:4. It is the name of a wadi that is still called by this name today, and this was evidently its original name.

We have found throughout our investigations that the Torah many times refers to the name of the encampments by a play on the original name in order to hint at what happened there.

The name Barnea, added to the other two places named Kadesh, might have been done in a similar way, in order to hint at what happened there by means of a play on words.

The word ברנע (Barnea) can be read בר נע, which can mean, "the one of wandering,"[4] or "without wandering." In Numbers 32:8, when Moses warns the tribes of Gad and Reuben not to make the same mistake that happened at the Sin of the Spies at Kadesh, he refers to it as Kadesh Barnea—the Kadesh that caused the decree of wandering.

In Deuteronomy 1:2, Moses, when rebuking the Israelites at Kadesh by the southwestern corner of Edom, hints to them that through their repentance, they could merit that this encampment be free of wandering. Indeed, it was, as they stayed there, through the merit of repentance, half the time of the exile.

4   Pointed out by Rabbi
    Pesach Bodenheimer.

# About the Author

Rabbi Alexander Hool grew up under the tutelage of his father, Rabbi Maurice Hool of Kingsbury, London, UK. He learned in Gateshead Yeshivah for many years under the direction of the Rosh Yeshivah, Rav Avrohom Gurwitz, and then moved to Israel where he has been studying in the Ponovezh Yeshivah and Kollel for over twenty years.

An eminent scholar, he has developed a particular expertise in history, dating, mathematics, and other unique and intriguing subjects. He is the author of the acclaimed work *Toras Yom VoLaylah* (on the complex halachic definitions of day, twilight, and night and their ramifications) and has published a fundamental study on ancient astronomy and its implications regarding the halachic dateline, as well as an analysis of the Murex Trunculus as a possible source of the ancient blue dye, *techelet*. Other recent publications include *Shiur HaShiurim* (a comprehensive investigation of the classification and calibration of measures and distances used in the Middle East before the Common Era), *The Challenge of Jewish History* (Mosaica, 2015), *Searching for Sinai* (Mosaica, 2018), and *Pharaoh* (Mosaica, 2020).

# The Challenge of Jewish History

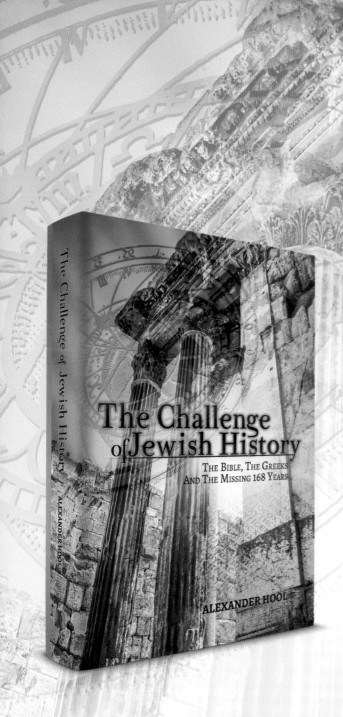

The conventional chronology of the Western world is in direct conflict with traditional Jewish sources over the history of...history. Incredibly, there is a gap of roughly 200 years—for instance, the Talmud says the Second Temple stood for roughly 400 years, while mainstream historians today conclude that it stood for almost 600 years. This conflict seems to question the accuracy of the entire Jewish tradition.

With fresh and startling astronomical, mathematical, and archaeological evidence, Rabbi Hool has charted new ground in his quest to find the solution to this ancient problem. With a subject of great significance and fascination to all those interested in history and a wealth of scholarship and sources to impress academics, this intriguing book gives us a new perspective on Jewish—and world—history.

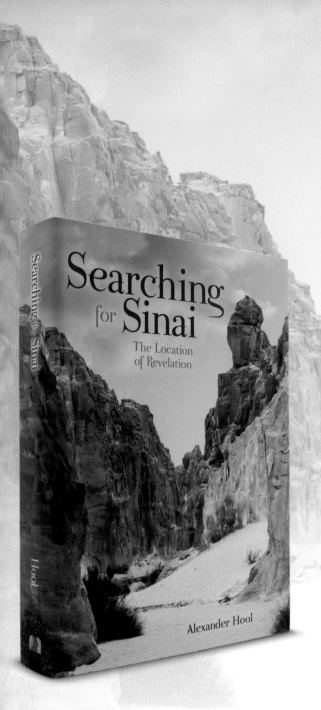

# Searching for Sinai

The most awesome moments of history were the crossing of the Red Sea and the giving of the Torah at Mount Sinai.

Ironically, the actual locations of both of these monumental events are shrouded in mystery. Generations of scholars and researchers have, since time immemorial, aspired to find these unique sites, however—although many theories have been propounded—none as yet have yielded any decisive archaeological evidence.

The Talmud attaches great importance to knowing the locations of these historical sites. Knowledge of their location brings to a more accurate understanding of the Biblical verses. At the same time, it paves the way to attaining a clearer picture of this crucial period in history.

In this unique and groundbreaking book, readers will be led to new and startling locations for both the crossing of the Red Sea and Mount Sinai.

# Pharaoh

Who was Pharaoh of the Bible?

A common scholarly identification for the Pharaoh of the Exodus is that of Ramesses the Great, from the 19th Dynasty of Egyptian kings. However, this identification poses problems. It does not fit in with the number of years stipulated by the Bible between the Exodus and the construction of the Second Temple by Darius the Great, the Persian monarch and ruler of the 27th Dynasty in Egypt. Furthermore, over the last couple of decades, archaeologists and researchers have uncovered a wealth of evidence contradicting this identification.

Another baffling problem is that traditional Jewish dating sets the beginning of the Egyptian Dynastic era at circa 2000 BCE, whereas the painstaking analysis of conventional chronologists yields a date of circa 3000 BCE.

In this fascinating study, bestselling author Rabbi Alexander Hool draws on fascinating research from many different disciplines as well as startling astronomical evidence to establish the convergence of a new Egyptian chronology in line with traditional Jewish dating. In addition, the path of investigation yields a surprising and penetrating insight into the setting of the Exodus, and this results in the contraction of Egyptian history by—incredibly—almost a thousand years!

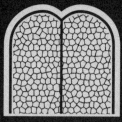

MOSAICA PRESS
BOOK PUBLISHERS

*Elegant, Meaningful & Bold*

info@MosaicaPress.com
www.MosaicaPress.com

The Mosaica Press team of
acclaimed editors and designers
is attracting some of the most
compelling thinkers and teachers
in the Jewish community today.
Our books are available around
the world.

HARAV YAACOV HABER
RABBI DORON KORNBLUTH